Squish, Sort, Paint & Build

Squish, Sort, Paint & Build

Over <u>200</u> Easy Learning Center Activities

By Sharon MacDonald

Illustrated by Rebecca Jones

gryphon house

Beltsville, Maryland

This book is dedicated to

Ariel, Victor, Megan, Jeremy

and all the other four year olds

who taught me so much

about teaching.

Copyright © 1996 Sharon MacDonald

Published by Gryphon House, Inc.
10726 Tucker Street, Beltsville, MD 20705

World Wide Web: http://www.ghbooks.com

Printed in the United States of America.

Cover: Graves Fowler Associates
Text Illustrations: Rebecca Jones

Library of Congress Cataloging-in-Publication Data

MacDonald, Sharon. 1942-
    Squish, sort, paint & build : over 200 easy learning center activities /
    by Sharon MacDonald ; illustrated by Rebecca Jones.
      p. cm.
    Includes index.
    ISBN 0-87659-180-2
    1. Early childhood education--Activity programs. 2. Creative activities
    and seat work. 3. Classroom learning centers. I. Title.
LB1139.35.A37M355 1996
372.21--dc20
                          96-9099
                          CIP

Table of Contents

Chapter 5
The Library Center 99

Chapter 7
The Motor Center 143

Chapter 6
The Manipulative Center .121

Chapter 8
The Music Center 165

Dear Teachers,

Although I have used centers for over 25 years, when I first set up a whole classroom where all the teaching was done through centers, I was a bit anxious. I set up my classroom in centers anyway, bit my lip and pressed forward with not much more than hope. The results surprised me. Centers worked! But not for very long. Why? After about a month, the children wanted change. It took me awhile to accept that centers needed to be revamped, revised. I concluded that change needed to happen often if centers were to work.

I also discovered that I often needed to justify the center approach I was using. It was noisier. The classroom often appeared to others to be in a perpetual state of motion. Structure is so often what we think we want to see. In a center-based classroom one must look closely if one is to find structure. The questioning, however, was good. It urged me to find out more about centers.

I spent a lot of time studying what children learned through a center-based approach to teaching. Then, I looked at the activities and tried to conclude what children could learn using the activity. That was good too, because what I found encouraged me even more.

Over the years I have experimented with many activities and ideas that could be shaped into a center-based approach. The activities and ideas really work. I know they do. I have used them all. I think you will find that they will enrich your classroom, enhance the learning that takes place there and they will excite your children, energizing them and you. I am certain they will add variety to your work. Enjoy trying them.

Sharon MacDonald

Sharon MacDonald

How to Use This Book

Helpful Tips to Make Centers Manageable and Child-directed

A good rule of thumb is to have two and one-half activities for each child working at the center. For example, if you have four children able to work at the center, you will need ten activities. This seems to be the magic number to keep children working productively and actively involved in what they are doing. If you have too many activities, the children get frustrated, feeling they won't be able to get to all of them. They may work too quickly and not enjoy the full benefit of the activities. On the other hand, if you have too few activities, it seems to create a battle zone over who gets which activity and when. Change the activities when the children seem to lose interest. If an activity goes unused for several days, it is time to change it. If an activity is popular, however, It needs to remain in the center for as long as it is used. If children are not interested in a particular activity, leave it out for a day or two then put it away. Bring it out 30 days later. You may be surprised at the result.

Locate each center in an appropriate place in the classroom. Some centers, such as the Construction Center, need large open spaces for building. The Library Center requires quiet spaces for reading and the Pouring Center needs to be located near a water source.

A good center management idea is to place each activity in a basket or dish pan with all the necessary component pieces included. Remember the activities in this book are open-ended; there is no right way to do any of them. For example, if the activity is a collage of shapes, then the basket containing the activity materials needs to contain a resealable bag with the paper shapes in them, a small bottle of glue, paper plates and a picture direction (rebus) that provides instructions to the children. They have everything they need to complete the project independently.

Use rebuses (step-by-step picture directions) as much as possible. They show children how to use the various materials and equipment properly. These simply drawn pictures invite the children to read along and to work at their own pace. Many of the illustrations that accompany the activities in this book can be easily converted into rebuses by adding written directions to the picture. Consider the ability level of the class when adding the words. Including activities with rebuses in centers is like having a second teacher in the classroom. The children become so completely involved in what they are doing that often they are not aware of the passage of time and of the presence of others in the classroom.

Make plans for clean up in advance. Have cleaning supplies handy: a broom, a dust pan, a small wet mop and newspaper for the children to cover their workspaces before they start. A garbage can, a wet sponge and smocks are also useful. This preparation saves you lots of headaches down the road when a small "disaster" occurs.

Chapter 1

The Art Center

● ●

The Art Center draws children to it like no other center in the classroom. It is a magic place where children find a place to express forms, images and structures. For many, it is the first time they will have the chance to work with their own unique ideas. Because the Art Center is for exploration—not necessarily for creating a finished product—children can work for a short time or long time, depending on each child's ability and temperament. They can choose the materials best suited for their ideas, their unique hand sizes and their moods or feelings at the time. When you encourage young children to experiment with a wide variety of art materials, they make their own experiences. It is empowering for them.

Art is about encouraging creativity in children. Open-ended art activities and materials give children opportunities to develop their own ideas and use their own designs. In doing this, they develop creative thinking skills and they learn to problem solve. In addition, language, reading, writing, math and motor skills develop while children are in the Art Center. Social skills and science skills also occur when children are left alone to find out things for themselves. Let's look at a sample of the skills that can be learned in the Art Center.

Language Development: Speaking and Listening

Talking and listening are vital skills. In the Art Center children talk and listen spontaneously when sharing thoughts, ideas and problem solving. Think of all the things there are to talk about when children work with playdough, for example: how it feels, smells, goes together, falls apart; big pieces, little pieces, how flat, or how soft it is. When children are painting at the easel, words such as runny, sparkle, slick, smooth, ooze and many others are used and explored. New vocabulary is developing. Words about gluing—sticky, stuck, gooey and tacky—evolve when children have dozens of opportunities to manipulate a glue bottle and work, sticking things together. Children want to talk to their friends and to share their discoveries.

● ●

Language Development: Reading and Writing

Reading and writing occur here, too. Children are encouraged to sign their works of art, just like famous artists sign theirs. Blank books are available in this Center in case a child wants to write a story about a painting he has created. Children are encouraged to make comments about their work and to write their thoughts and ideas on paper. The writings can be attached to their paintings. Books about famous artists' works are available in the Center so the children can become familiar with different artists' styles. Children interact with print in the Art Center by using rebuses to give them directions. These picture directions simply get children started using the materials. The children work the activity by "reading" the rebus.

Physical Development

When children cut with scissors, paint with brushes, pound playdough, open glue bottles and scribble with crayons, they are developing hand-eye coordination, hand manipulation and pincher control. When children work at the easel and move through the Art Center, they are learning about their bodies in space; and about using both sides of their bodies to accomplish a task.

Math

Math occurs naturally when children use, repeat and extend patterns, as with a stringing activity, for example: one piece of straw, one paper circle, one piece of straw, one paper circle and so on. Patterns are basic to math. Gluing precut, geometrical, paper shapes, painting on them and stringing them together teach children basic geometry. When they work with playdough or clay, children are exposed to part/whole relationships, with more/less and with thick/thin. There is no need to have a math lesson. The activities themselves become the math teacher.

Science

Science can be a part of the Center when children mix and make their own colors. Children can use the scientific method while working. They can state the problem or question: "What will happen if I paint with the blue over the yellow?" They can state their hypotheses-predictions. "I think it will turn green." They can test this by painting as they have stated. When they observe the finished work, they compare results to see if their hypotheses-predictions were valid. This is an easy way to teach science. When children glue glitter to paper, they observe causality (if I do this, then that happens). The world becomes less mysterious. Magical thinking, a common phenomenon in young children, is replaced by knowledge about how things happen. Gravity, for example, can be explored as the paint runs down the page, while the children are painting. They also can learn about the properties of matter when they work with the various materials that are available to them in the Art Center.

Social Development

Children learn to share materials, work together on projects and to take turns doing activities. The Center offers children the chance to make choices and decisions for themselves. As children come to the Center, choose an activity "read" the picture directions, work the activity and return it to the shelf, they are practicing good social skills. They develop a sense of self-confidence, as well, by doing things for themselves. They are in charge.

Creating the Art Center

Since we know how important a well planned, well organized and well managed Art Center is, we need to look at how we go about making it a place where learning will take place. The first consideration is deciding where to put the Art Center in the classroom. The ideal spot is close to a source of water and a sink. If the water source is down the hall, have two dishpans: one with a little soapy water and the other with clear water. Add paper towels, and you have a place to prewash the children's hands before heading down the hall with them to finish the job in the bathroom. Have a small bucket, with a soapy sponge, for spills. If you don't have a sink, include a couple of liquid trash buckets. These would allow the children to toss their liquid trash. These would be emptied by the teacher at the end of the day.

The second consideration is the traffic pattern in your classroom. Children walking through the Art Center on the way to the Block Center invites disaster. So, locate the Art Center away from the main traffic flow.

The third consideration is a good light source. A window close by is optimum; it makes the Art Center a more inviting area, but it is not essential. If a window is not available, place the Center where you have the best light.

Fourth, is the floor covering. Tile is the best, but if you have carpeting, use a shower curtain-liner or a painter's drop cloth to cover the areas most likely to take the most spills and messes. It is not ideal, but it works to protect the carpet.

The last consideration is the furniture. You will need a table and chairs on which the children can sit and work and a two-sided, free-standing easel. Place the easel on a shower curtain-liner beneath the easel and the drying rack. You also will need low, open shelving to house your selection of art activities from which the children will choose. A place to dry all of those creations will be helpful, too. The best method, that takes up the least amount of space, is a multilevel box construction. Get five or six, low profile cardboard boxes at the grocery store. Remove the same side of each box and stack them one on top of the other. Have all the removed sides facing the same direction. Tape the boxes together at the sides and back. The box construction can be covered with decorative self-adhesive paper, providing more stability. Now, you have a number of vertical shelves on which to slide the children's "gluey" creations for drying (see illustration).

Self-directed Activities

Because you want the children to make choices about the materials with which they work—the media that interests them—offer them a wide variety of activities from which to choose. The ultimate goal is for the children to develop the skills discussed earlier, a variety of activities is necessary to attract each child to the Center. The reason for the diversity is that some will learn to use scissors by cutting paper strips, others by cutting magazine pictures and still others by cutting playdough.

A good rule of thumb is to have two and one-half activities for each child working at the Art Center table. One or two children can also be in the center working at the easel. For example, if you have four children able to work at the table, you will need to have ten choices of activities on the open shelving from which the children can choose. Does this sound like a lot of work for a busy teacher? Well, it really isn't. Actually once the Art Center is set up, the activities stay out for as long as the children are choosing them. That could be for two weeks, two months or maybe the whole year. Replace them with new activities as needed. Teacher time is reduced, over the long run, as the children interact with and learn through the environment.

Another good management idea is to place each art activity in a basket with all the necessary component pieces included. Remember these activities are open-ended. There is not a right way to do any of them. Let's take an example. If you are doing a shape collage activity, and it is a choice on the Art Center shelf, then the basket containing the activity needs to contain all the components needed to complete a shape collage. You would have a resealable bag with the paper shapes in them, a small bottle of glue, paper plates and a picture direction that provides instructions to the children. They have everything they need to complete the project.

Clean Up

Make plans for clean up in advance. Have cleaning implements handy: a broom, a dust pan, a small wet mop and newspaper for the children to cover their workspaces before they start. A garbage can, a wet sponge, and smocks are useful, too, for messy choices. These preparations save you lots of headaches down the road when a small "disaster" occurs.

Learning, through a carefully planned and prepared environment means that we must look carefully at each activity placed in the Center. You might want to use the checklist that follows to see if your Art Center activity choices enhance creativity.

Creativity Checklist

✓ Can the child do something with the activity? Is it hands-on?

✓ Can the child use her or his own ideas, thoughts and methods?

✓ Are there opportunities for discovery?

✓ Is the activity meaningful to the child and does it fit into his or her world?

✓ Is the activity age, developmentally and individually appropriate?

✓ Is the activity self-directed?

✓ Who does most of the work, the child or the teacher?

✓ Can the child work for a short time or for a long time?

All of the activities require that the child prepare the workspace for use. After the child selects the activity to be used, newspaper is placed on the workspace by the child. The child puts on a smock. After completing the activity, all activity components are washed and the basket containing all the materials is returned to the shelf for use by other children. The newspaper is tossed and the painting, or other artwork, is set aside to dry. It is very important that the children learn these expectations and perform these tasks with a minimum of teacher intervention.

Useful Art Center Additions

These additions add interest to the Art Center activities. Substitutions and additions of these items offer variety and change.

Things to add to one pint of mixed tempera paint:

2 Tbs. corn syrup	to make it slimy
1/2 tsp. sand	to make it gritty
1 Tbs. flour	to make it lumpy
1 tsp. glycerin	to make it slippery
1 Tbs. sawdust	to make it rough
1/2 cup sugar	to make it shiny
1/2 cup salt	to make is sparkly (use this immediately)
1/4 cup liquid starch	to make it creamy

Things to use as bases for art projects:

newspaper	meat trays
fingerpaint paper	cardboard
shoe box tops	construction paper
sandpaper	paper sacks
leftover laminating film	computer paper
egg carton lids	aluminum foil
toilet paper cylinders	fast food cartons
paper plates	wrapping paper
large junk mail envelopes	

Things to cut:

playdough	old magazines
straws	hay
crepe paper streamers	paper strips
meat trays	catalogs
old postcards	old placemats

Things to use for paintbrushes:

sponges	feathers
twigs	leaves (ferns are best)
whisk brooms	strings tied on sticks
dish mops	roll-on bottles
pot scrubbers	feather dusters
squeeze bottles	cotton swabs
toothbrushes	chop sticks
paddle balls	vegetable brushes
paint rollers	straws
eyedroppers	cotton balls
fly swatters	scrubbing pads

Things to use instead of paint:

food coloring and water	watercolors
Epsom salt	watery glue and crayon shavings
toothpaste	watery glue and sawdust
Kosher salt	whipped white detergent, such as Ivory

Things to use for printing:

wood scraps	leaves
empty spools	toy cars
jar lids	box lids
kitchen gadgets	corks
shells	cookie cutters
fake fur	dominoes
hands, fingers and feet	pot scrubbers
keys	large buttons
marker caps	sponges

Cotton Ball Painting

3+

Language & Physical development

Children develop and practice pincher control (thumb and first finger use) and fine motor control with this activity and, they experiment with texture and color.

Materials

✓ basket
✓ cotton balls
✓ assorted paper
✓ paint
✓ newspaper
✓ resealable sandwich bag
✓ 3 clothespins
✓ 3 small margarine tubs

What to do

Insert many cotton balls in a resealable sandwich bag.

Have lots of paper available (try different kinds of paper like grocery bag paper, old manila folders and envelopes that have been cut at the edge and laid flat).

Add three clothespins and a rebus to the basket; place the basket on the shelf.

On another shelf, accessible to the children, have three, small margarine tubs into which you have poured small amounts of paint (keep extra paint handy to restock the tubs).

The child selects the activity and places the three tubs on the workspace.

The child squeezes the clothespins to capture a cotton ball, dips it into the paint and paints (or prints) with the cotton ball on paper. When the child is finished exploring the activity, she tosses the cotton balls and newspaper, returns the tubs to the shelf and puts her creation aside to dry. She returns the basket to the shelf.

Note: Your local pharmacist tosses away vast amounts of cotton every day. Ask her to save it for you. Cut the cotton into small pieces for this activity. You also can use pompoms just as you would use cotton balls in this activity.

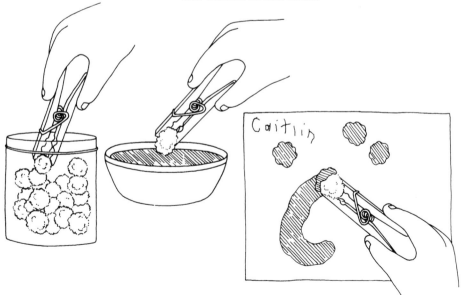

Feather Painting

3+

Language & Physical development

Science

This is a favorite activity of children, and it offers many opportunities for them to problem solve. Each child will approach the task differently.

Materials

✓ basket
✓ turkey feathers
✓ small flat tray

✓ newspaper
✓ variety of paper
✓ paint

What to do

Place one turkey feather, lots of paper (I like to use paper cut from brown grocery bags) and the rebus in a basket.

Place a small tray of paint (dark brown paint seems to offer the most interesting contrast on brown grocery bags) on a shelf easily accessible to the children. Be sure to mix plenty of paint to replenish the tray.

The child places the small tray of paint on the workspace.

When children use this activity you see each child work a little differently. The children dip the feather, sometimes the pointed end, sometimes the feathered end, and they draw or paint with the feather.

Some of the children learn they can make interesting designs when they slap the feathered end onto the paper (they also learn that sometimes small paint spots appear all around the workspace and on their faces). They learn, also, that a sponge is necessary to clean it up.

When a child has finished, part of the job is to put back the paint tray and wash and dry the feather.

It is exciting watching children explore and discover with this activity. Try other types of feathers and compare the results.

Follow the Leader Painting

3+

Language & Social development

This activity helps children develop language skills and it gives them a structured, useful reason to talk to each other. Also, it makes them aware of how important clear directions are and how equally important it is to listen.

Materials

✓ easel
✓ paper
✓ paint and brushes

What to do

When two children have chosen to paint at the two-sided easel, have one child be the leader and the other the follower.

The leader starts to paint and describes what she is doing and what color she is using while she is working.

As she works and describes, the other child follows the leader's directions trying to do exactly what the leader says without looking at the leader's work.

Have the children reverse roles. This is very challenging and lots of fun, especially when the children compare their two finished works of art afterwards.

Sparkle Art

3+

Language development

Science

This activity invites children to experiment with pastel colors and with depth as a quality of art (overcoming the flatness that exemplifies their work by bringing a third dimension into play).

Materials

✓ basket
✓ plastic squeeze bottles
✓ measuring cup
✓ salt
✓ paper plates or sheets of cardboard
✓ newspaper
✓ bowl and spoon
✓ flour
✓ food coloring

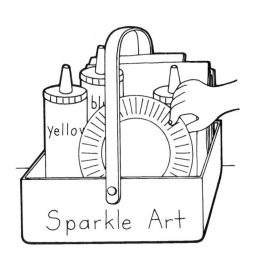

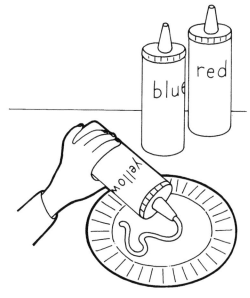

What to do

Collect three plastic squeeze bottles that have caps (like ketchup or mustard bottles).

Mix together in a bowl, one cup of all-purpose flour, one cup of salt and one cup of water colored with food coloring. Make three different color mixtures.

Stir the mixtures well and pour each color into one of the squeeze bottles. Save the extra colored water for use later to replenish the plastic bottles. If the mixture is too moist, add more flour.

Put the bottles, paper plates or sheets of cardboard and the rebus in a basket on the shelf.

The child squeezes the mixture onto the paper plates in a design.

The discovery takes place when the creations are dry. The mixture dries hard, and it sparkles and shines.

Glitter Painting

This activity teaches children patience. They will not be able to see the end result of their work until their work has dried. The drying process takes about a day.

Materials

- ✓ quart jar
- ✓ glitter
- ✓ paintbrush
- ✓ liquid starch
- ✓ tablespoon
- ✓ black or dark blue paper

What to do

Fill a quart jar with liquid starch and two tablespoons of glitter.

Place the jar and a paintbrush at the easel.

Place large sheets of black or dark blue paper on the easel.

When the children come to the easel, initially they must stir the starch/glitter mixture with the brush each time they make a paint stroke (since the glitter settles to the bottom of the jar rapidly).

When the child is through, the creation will look like a very wet piece of paper, with a little glitter showing through the wetness. When it dries, however, the painting will be covered with glitter only; the wetness (provided by the starch base) will no longer be visible.

Note: Dry the paper flat since the starch will make the paper brittle.

Marble Art

This is an exciting activity because all the work is done inside a closed container, and nothing is seen until the child is finished. Children can predict what is going to happen inside the can.

Materials

- ✓ basket
- ✓ sectioned plate
- ✓ 3 plastic spoons
- ✓ marbles
- ✓ tennis ball can or something similar
- ✓ paper, cut to fit inside can

Put paper in the can.

Put the lid on the can.

Add painted marbles.

Shake the can.

What to do

Put the can, the marbles, the paper and the rebus of the activity in a basket.

Put small amounts of different colored paint in each compartment of the plate. Place the plate on a shelf that is easily accessible to the children. Be sure to mix plenty of extra paint.

The child puts the paper in the tennis can, puts the marbles in the paint, uses a spoon to remove one, two or three marbles from the paint and drops the marble(s) into the can.

The child puts the lid on and shakes it. This can be repeated as many times as the child would like. When the child is finished, the paper is removed and examined by the child looking for effects.

The activity can be repeated with the same paper or with another sheet of paper.

Sprinkle Art

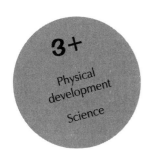

3+

Physical
development

Science

This is an excellent activity to increase and to develop tactile awareness by exposing the children to different textures.

Materials

✓ 4 large, clear salt shakers
✓ fine sawdust, sand, salt and fine, crushed rock
✓ paper plates   ✓ glue
✓ basket   ✓ tray or box lid

What to do

Collect four large, clear salt shakers (or Parmesan cheese shakers).

Collect fine sawdust, sand, salt and fine, crushed rock (or use bird grit; it can be purchased from a pet store).

Make a design on paper with glue.

Sprinkle.

Shake off excess.

Fill each shaker with a different material. Place the shakers in the basket with paper plates, a container of glue and a rebus.

Have a "shake-off" tray or box lid close by. The child works inside the "shake-off" tray.

She uses the glue, squeezing a design on a paper plate, then sprinkles one of the materials over the glue.

When the child is through designing with the glue, she shakes off the excess material into the tray and sets the creation aside to dry, empties the "shake-off" tray into the trash and returns the basket to the shelf.

Classical Music Art

3+

Language & Social development

This is an excellent activity to introduce quiet time in the classroom or to maintain it when the class has settled down. It focuses the children's attention on listening.

Materials

✓ butcher paper
✓ tape
✓ crayons or markers
✓ classical music

What to do

Tape a piece of butcher paper to a wall, on the floor or beneath a table in the classroom.

Play a classical music tape or record ("The Grand Canyon Suite" is an excellent and dramatic choice).

The children draw with the crayons or markers to the music, trying to express the feeling, intensity, rhythm and mood of the music. Encourage them to focus on the sounds they hear and to move their drawing motions with the music.

Record Player Art

3+

Language, Physical & Social development

Once you put out this activity, you will not be able to put it away. There will be at least one child working all of the time.

Materials

✓ old record player
✓ paper cut into circles
✓ basket

✓ cardboard circle
✓ markers

What to do

Purchase an old record player and remove the needle arm (flea markets or garage sales are good places to look).

Cut out a cardboard circle about one inch larger in diameter than the turntable.

Cut out lots of paper the same size as the cardboard circle.

Push the cardboard circle onto the turntable center post (the post should show through the cardboard).

Place the record player in an out-of-the-way spot in the Art Center, close to an electrical outlet.

Place a basket with paper, markers and a rebus on the art shelf. The child chooses the basket, takes it to the record player, places a piece of art paper over the post and presses it down. She turns the turntable on and uses the markers to draw on the moving circle.

Note: To broaden and extend interest, put the record player in a deep cardboard box and let the children use eyedroppers to drop paint on the art paper, spinning on the turntable.

Coffee Filter Art

3+

Physical development

Science

This activity offers many teachable moments. Among them: a discussion of color-mixing, making predictions and similarities and differences. It also develops fine motor skills.

Materials

✓ large coffee filters
✓ small jars
✓ newspaper

✓ food coloring
✓ eyedroppers
✓ basket

What to do

Use the largest coffee filters you can buy—the ones for big coffee urns. They can be purchased inexpensively at a restaurant supply store. If those are not available, use regular size filters.

Put small amounts of water in each jar and color the water liberally with food coloring. Put on the lid tightly.

Put the jars, eyedroppers, filters and a rebus of the activity in a basket on the art shelf.

The child chooses the activity, covers the workspace with newspaper, spreads out one filter (or, if the child prefers, folds it) and uses the eyedropper to squeeze droplets of colored water on the filter to create a design.

Peanut Shell Printing

3+

Language & Physical development

This is a wonderful activity to show children the usefulness of throwaway items. It is also a fun activity to follow snack time.

Materials

✓ basket
✓ divided dinner plate
✓ peanut shells
✓ paper, cut into circles

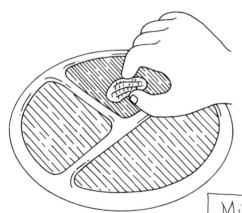

What to do

Place a few of the shells, the paper and a rebus in a basket on the art shelf.

On another shelf place divided dinner plate with small amounts of paint in each compartment.

The child places the divided plate on the workspace.

He puts the shells in the paint and prints on the paper. Afterward, the shells are tossed, and more shells are added for the next child.

Note: If the children have difficulty making a clear print, reverse the process and paint the top of the shell. Lay the paper over the shells, pressing the paper gently on the shells, making a shell imprint.

Tennis Shoe Printing

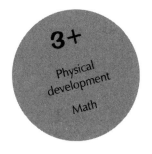

3+

Physical development

Math

Tennis shoe printing gives children opportunities to look for patterns, finding characteristics that make shoe prints similar and different. Finding similarities and differences is a fundamental skill, critical to most learning.

Materials

✓ basket
✓ 3 flat trays
✓ paper

✓ tennis shoes
✓ paint
✓ newspaper

What to do

Find tennis shoes with different designs on the soles, the more diverse the designs the better. Small tennis shoes are better than large ones for this activity. Parents are a good source of supply.

Place two or three tennis shoes in a basket with many large sheets of paper. Include picture directions (rebus). Put the basket on the shelf in the Art Center.

On another easily assessable shelf, place three flat trays into which the tennis shoe(s) can be dipped.

Pour small amounts of different colors of paint into the trays (one color per tray). Provide plenty of premixed paint nearby to refill the trays.

The child selects a tennis shoe, dips it into one of the trays and prints on the paper. She repeats the printing until she is finished with the activity.

Cleaning up is the child's responsibility. She rinses the shoe soles, dries them, sets the trays aside for the next child and returns the basket to the shelf. She also sets aside her artwork to dry. The newspaper is thrown away. When the tennis shoe print is dry, the child examines it to see the patterns.

Note: If you have the space for a large mural, try using different sizes of tennis shoes.

Bubble Wrap Printing

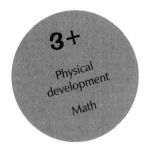

3+

Physical development

Math

Modeling how to recycle is very important. This activity also teaches children about the relative sizes of things. Children are encouraged to use words like large, medium and small.

Materials

✓ box
✓ glue
✓ paint
✓ paintbrush
✓ basket

✓ bubble wrap
✓ tape
✓ baby food jar
✓ paper

What to do

Collect a box about one foot square by one foot deep.

Glue different sample sizes of bubble wrap to five sides of the box. Use the sixth side as the base. Cut the bubble wrap in one-foot squares; glue them to the sides of the box.

Tape all of the seams where the bubble wrap meets the corners and edges of the box. Use plastic tape. When this creation is dry, you have a bubble box.

Pour a small amount of paint in a baby food jar and put on the lid.

Put the jar with the paint, a paintbrush, lots of paper and picture directions in a basket on the shelf. Place the bubble wrap box beside the basket.

The child places the bubble box on the workspace along with the brush. He brushes the paint either on the large, medium or small bubble wrap.

Next he lays a sheet of paper over the painted area and presses gently.

He pulls off the paper to see his design. He can print several times without repainting the bubble wrap.

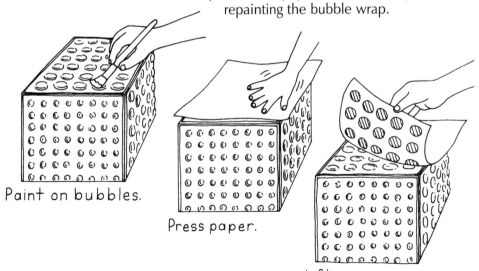

Paint on bubbles.

Press paper.

Lift paper.

Note: there is little need for clean up since the reprinting removes the most of the paint from the surface of the bubble wrap. The paint between the bubbles is not a problem since it dries. Even if you use a different color of paint the next day, it will not mix with the previous day's color when the children make a print.

Tissue Paper Collage

3+

Language development

Math

This activity develops and improves, figure and ground perception. Cut out circles, squares, triangles and ovals from different color tissue paper, about 2" wide. Collect lots of paper to use as the base for the activity. The tissue shapes are applied to the construction paper, making a collage.

Materials

✓ tissue paper, cut into shapes
✓ resealable plastic bag
✓ paper
✓ small jar of liquid starch
✓ basket

What to do

Place the tissue paper shapes in a resealable plastic bag, one handful at a time.

Place the bag of tissue shapes, the paper, a small jar of liquid starch, a brush and a rebus in a basket on the shelf.

First, the child brushes the starch on the paper used as the base.

Then, he places tissue shapes in the starch, brushing those with starch.

He applies more tissue shapes in this fashion randomly around the paper base, overlapping the shapes. This results in an overlay of colors and shapes, creating interesting and colorful effects.

Brush starch on paper.

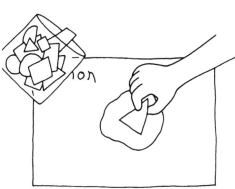

Put a shape in the starch.

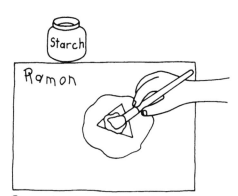

Brush starch on the shape.

Feather Collage

3+

Physical
development

Science

The children must do some problem solving when working with the following materials. They have to come up with a way to hold the cylinder while working. Also they will find the glue sticks the feathers to their fingers and they have to figure out how to transfer them to the cylinder.

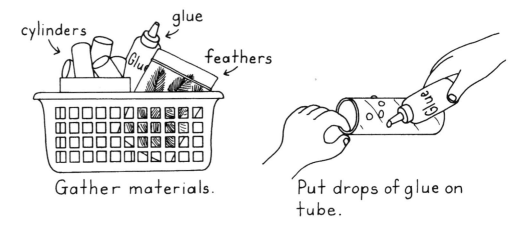

Gather materials.

Put drops of glue on tube.

Press feathers into glue.

Materials

✓ feathers
✓ toilet paper cylinders
✓ resealable plastic bag
✓ glue
✓ basket

What to do

Collect feathers of any kind (if you have a feather duster, you can recycle the feathers by using them for this activity) and toilet paper cylinders.

Place the feathers in a resealable plastic bag. Put it and the toilet paper cylinders, a glue bottle and a rebus in a basket. Place the basket on the shelf.

The child chooses the activity, glues the feathers onto the cylinder in any design he chooses.

Note: To dry the feathered cylinders, place a tree branch in a can of rocks in the classroom. Slip the cylinders on the branches to dry. The children see their "birds" roosting in the tree.

Crayon Muffins

3+

Science

This is a fun way to recycle those small, broken pieces of crayons and a great sorting activity. Children will enjoy using the recycled crayons for drawing.

Materials

✓ muffin tins or candy molds
✓ broken crayon pieces
✓ oven at 250° F

What to do

Collect two or three muffin tins or candy molds suitable for heating in an oven.

Gather all of the broken crayon pieces and have the children peel the paper from them.

After peeling, ask the children to sort them by color. Let the children choose how their recycled crayons will look; that is, multicolored or one color.

Break up the selected crayons into smaller pieces and place them in the muffin tin, filling the cups to the top.

Preheat the oven to 250° F. Heat the crayons for ten minutes, checking every five minutes, to see if they are soft to the touch but not liquid (if they become liquid the colors will mix together too completely, and the multicolored, interesting effects will be reduced). Set them aside to cool. Turn out the crayons from the muffin tin, and let the children use them to draw on paper.

Note: Before baking the crayon cookies, remove most of the black and purple crayons. These two colors will dominate the crayon muffin if the crayons accidentally get too hot in the oven.

License Plate Rubbing

3+
Language & Physical development
Science

This activity improves letter and number recognition and enhances fine motor skills in young children.

Materials

✓ old license plates
✓ sheets of paper
✓ peeled crayons
✓ basket

What to do

Collect old license plates (flea markets often have many of them for sale), peeled crayons and sheets of paper.

Place them in a basket on the art shelf.

The child chooses the activity, places the paper over the license plate and rubs over the license plate using the sides of the crayons. The numbers and letters appear on the paper.

Note: You can rub over coins, leaves, fabric, anything with an interesting surface.

Tire Rubbing

3+
Language & Physical development
Science

This activity is excellent for the children to examine patterns.

Materials

✓ half a tire with tread
✓ paper
✓ peeled crayons
✓ basket

What to do

You will need half of a tire with tread (a crosscut wood saw can be used to cut the tire if it is not steel belted; use a hack saw if the tire is steel belted).

Place the tire on a table or on the floor.

Place a basket with a rebus of the activity, peeled crayons and paper on the art shelf.

The child takes the basket to the tire, "reads" the rebus and does the activity by laying paper over the tire tread and rubbing the paper with the side of a crayon.

The tire tread pattern is duplicated and examined.

Playdough

3+

Language & Physical development

Science

Pounding, poking, rolling and pushing playdough improves small muscle control. It is also a great tension releaser.

Materials

✓ spatula, bowl, whisk or spoon, measuring cups and spoons
✓ electric skillet   ✓ flour
✓ cream of tartar   ✓ vegetable oil
✓ salt   ✓ food coloring
✓ water   ✓ plastic resealable bag
✓ plastic knife   ✓ rolling pin
✓ cookie cutters   ✓ plastic placemat

What to do

Mix 1 cup of flour with 2 tsp. of cream of tartar, 1/2 cup of salt, 1 Tbs. of oil and 1 cup of colored water in a bowl with a whisk or spoon.

Preheat the electric skillet to 300° F. Pour the mixture into the skillet and stir using the spatula. Keep stirring until the mixture forms a ball and it pulls away from the sides of the skillet.

When it is done, turn it out on the counter.

When it is cool, knead it until it is smooth. Leave it out until it reaches room temperature.

Store the playdough in a plastic resealabe bag or a large margarine tub.

Place the playdough in a basket along with a plastic knife, a rolling pin, cookie cutters and a plastic placemat.

The child plays with the playdough, cutting shapes and making designs until he is finished.

Styrofoam Stringing

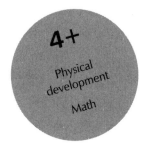

4+

Physical
development

Math

This is excellent for developing the small muscle groups of the hand and wrist that are necessary for writing.

Materials

- ✓ styrofoam peanuts
- ✓ toothpick
- ✓ scissors
- ✓ basket
- ✓ string or yarn
- ✓ glue
- ✓ masking tape

What to do

Cut the string or yarn into 15" lengths.

Make a needle and thread for stringing. To do this, squeeze a 1/4" glue line on a toothpick. Place one end of the string on the glue. The toothpick will serve as a needle, pulling the string through the styrofoam pieces. Make many "needles and threads" for stringing as you can, since this is a very popular activity.

At the other end, fold a piece of masking tape across the string. Write the child's name on the tape (the folded piece of tape also will serve to keep the styrofoam from sliding off the end of the string). Place several "needles and threads," a plastic bag full of styrofoam peanuts and a rebus in a basket on the art shelf.

The child uses the toothpick as a needle and pushes it through the styrofoam peanuts to make a stringing.

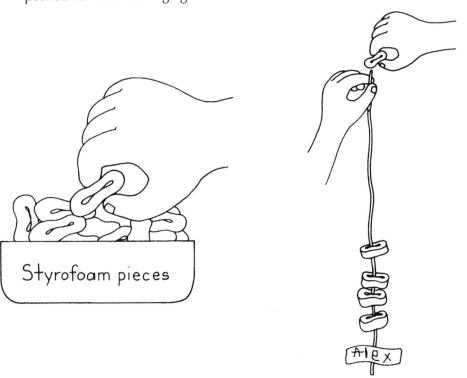

Styrofoam pieces

Alex

Box Construction

4+

Physical development

Math

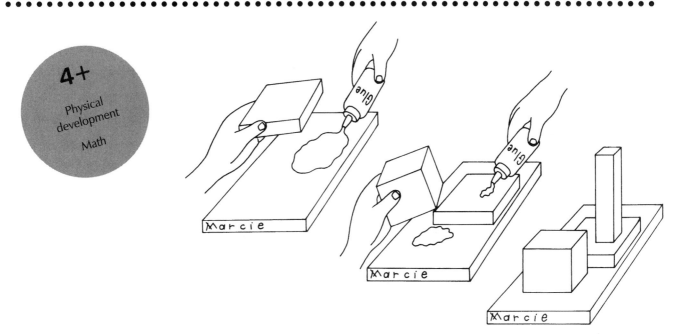

This activity punctuates the importance of planning, and it demonstrates the effect of gravity if a child's planning is poor.

Materials

✓ boxes smaller than a shoe box
✓ shoe boxes
✓ basket

✓ tape
✓ glue
✓ shoe box lids

What to do

Collect boxes that are smaller than a shoe box. Tape them closed as you collect them. Collect shoe boxes also. When you have a plentiful supply, you are ready.

Place a basket of small boxes with a container of glue and a rebus on the art shelf.

Beside the basket, place one or two shoe box lids and one or two shoe box bottoms giving the children a choice as to which they will use as a base on which for their constructions. Some will want to build inside the box bottom, others will use the top, while still others will want to turn over the bottom and build on it. There is no correct way. The children use the boxes, designing their own construction, gluing their constructions together box by box.

Plan a place for their creations to dry.

Note: After the box constructions have dried, they can be painted.

Rolled Paper Construction

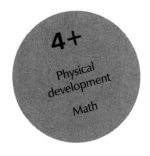

4+

Physical development

Math

This activity requires well developed, fine motor skills. It is very popular in the classroom, however it is difficult for very young children.

Materials

✓ old magazines
✓ pencil
✓ tape
✓ basket

What to do

Prepare paper rolls ahead of time by cutting apart old magazines. Roll each page on a pencil, making long, slender rolls.

Tape the rolls closed at both ends. Make hundreds of them. Purchase rolls of inexpensive, clear plastic tape (in dispensers).

Place the rolled paper, tape and a rebus in a basket on the art shelf.

The child chooses the activity and tapes the rolled paper together in a three-dimension construction.

Plan a place for the constructions to be placed until the children take them home. It is fun to make as a class construction, as well.

Note: You can make larger rolls using newspaper. This is a fun and challenging activity to do at a parent's meeting (they can build a construction, too).

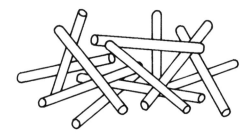

Tape it to other rolls to make a construction.

rolled magazine pages

Choose a paper roll.

Chapter 2

The Block Center

Blocks are among the most useful learning tools. Through block play and block construction children experiment with their own ideas—growing, learning and developing skills in the process. This makes a Block Center essential in the classroom. Most curriculum areas can be taught through block play. When children play with blocks, specially in small groups, they learn about mathematical concepts, science, social studies, art and language arts (which encompass reading, writing and language development). Social, emotional and physical developments also are enhanced through block play. The following lists each area mentioned above and exactly what and how children learn through block play.

Art

Art is creative expression. It is expressed in many different ways; architecture is one of them. Indeed, it is the oldest of the fine arts. Many people have expressed themselves artistically through the buildings they build. Children learn about many architectural styles when using blocks. When they look at photographs of architectural styles from throughout the world they may be inspired to create different types of structures. Artistic values—perceptions about symmetry and balance—emerge as the children work. They learn that blocks can be used to symbolize ideas and forms from their own imagination. The children also have opportunities to create, repeat and to extend patterns.

Language Development

Reading and writing occur when the children make signs to attach to their constructions. To take an example from my own classroom, a child wrote: "Go over the road slow so it will not fall down." The other children using the Center could not read the individual words, but they could discern enough to follow the directions. Reading was occurring. The road did not fall down! The children also make labels to attach to their buildings. I had one child make a large yellow "M" on an index card. She affixed it to the structure.

She told everyone that it was McDonald's, for hamburgers. Another way to encourage reading is by using rebuses (picture directions with words, too). The children are encouraged to read pictures to understand what to do. Gradually, they associate the words and pictures, and they learn to read the words alone. By differentiating between the various block shapes, the children learn about similarities and differences. Eventually, they will be able to differentiate between letters. Adding blank writing books to the Block Center gives the children opportunities to write stories about their structures. Language development evolves when the children exchange ideas, plans and ask questions about block building.

Math

Unit blocks were created by Carolyn Pratt in the late 1800s. They were and still are made in direct mathematical proportions because of her belief that. Because of the exact mathematical proportions of the blocks, the children become aware of fractions, part/whole relationships, and of inequality or equality by working with the various sizes, shapes and proportions of the blocks.

When they work with the blocks children become aware of height: "My building is six blocks tall. Yours is four. Mine is taller." They become aware of weight. At clean up time, carrying three blocks to the shelf requires less work than carrying ten. Children develop, as well, a sense of width, length and depth when placing blocks in structures. They learn symmetry, order, pattern and, through more complex designs, mapping. Blocks can be used for measuring other areas, spaces and things in the classroom. Math essentials are learned in all block center activities.

Physical Development

Block play is an excellent way for children to develop eye-hand coordination and visual perception. Children develop an awareness of their bodies in the space around them when working with other children in the Block Center.

Social Development

Children develop a feeling of self-confidence when they work in the Block Center. They feel in charge of their own learning—empowered. They learn to cooperate, and they gain respect for others as they work with blocks. They gain confidence. When you have seen a child struggle to find a way to make one big block sit atop some of the smaller ones and finally get it done, you see a child who becomes willing to take on new challenges.

Social Studies

Social studies occur when the children use props such as family figures, community workers or farm characters to enrich their block play. Children learn about people, their activities, their roles and their work. They act out different social roles, either alone or with others, in the different settings they have constructed in the Block Center. When we see a child sitting in the middle of his construction pretending to be a bus driver, we know he has some understanding of what a bus driver does to make a living.

Science

When children create a seesaw construction with blocks, what do they learn from it? They learn about leverage—the lever and how it works—and they learn about other simple machines like the inclined plane, which includes the wedge and the ramp. Momentum is observed when a child rolls a car down a ramp. They learn about gravity when their buildings fall down. Children become aware of the physical qualities of blocks when they find that they can roll round blocks faster than square ones, that triangular blocks are harder to balance than square ones. They use inductive reasoning when they learn block building through trial and error. With blocks, a child uses all her mental powers—reasoning-out relationships; drawing conclusions—to invent things for herself. The block center is a wonderful way to introduce and to develop and extend many scientific concepts.

Creating the Block Center

Knowing that all kinds of learning takes place in the Block Center makes it one of the most exciting places in the classroom. It is essential and basic; yet, it is avoided by many teachers. There have been several objections voiced by teachers with whom I have spoken over the years: noise, the danger of blocks used to hit or to throw and clean up. These potential problems can be mediated if the environment is prepared to avoid them. Let's look at a way to prepare the Block Center so these problems are avoided altogether or substantially minimized. First, have enough blocks. Think of having 22 children and 19 cookies at snack time; it is the same with blocks. There must be enough for the children to share, yet sufficient to allow them to create whatever structure they have in mind.

With seven to ten three year olds, about 215 blocks are needed; with the same number of four year olds, about 350; and five year olds, about 475. The more blocks, the more elaborate the children will make their constructions. Because the frustration level is reduced by having enough blocks, the tendency to be noisy or to fight is greatly reduced.

Have enough space for the Block Center. If children are working on top of one another, their buildings tend to be knocked down, feelings get hurt and "war" breaks out. To keep children from knocking down each other's constructions, place a tape line about two feet from the shelves on which the blocks are stored and retrieved. This is the walking zone or no building zone. You might want to label it as such. Children can get to the blocks easily, avoiding the work of others.

To help with the noise, use a low-napped rug. Not only does it define the Block Center boundary for you, but it decreases the noise when the buildings come tumbling down. And they will!

To help with clean up, place silhouettes of each block shape on the block shelves on which each block is stored. Have the children match the block with the silhouette. This says to the children that each block has its place on the shelf. The children can play games to make clean up fun. Have them give each other assignments like: "You pick up three triangles and four switches. I'll pick up seven squares." (See the Clean-Up Activity Cards on page 70).

Use rebuses as much as possible. They show the children how to use the various materials and equipment properly. These simply drawn picture directions invite the children to "read" along and to work at their own pace. Many of the illustrations that accompany the activities in this book can be converted easily into rebuses. All you need to do is to add written directions to the illustrations. Consider the ability level of the class when adding the words. It is also a big help to give the children a five-minute warning before clean up time, then the children will have time to conclude their work. It has been my experience that the children appreciate this consideration and they are more cooperative when block play must come to an end.

Limits are important; they work best if the children establish them. If the limits are owned by the children, they are followed more enthusiastically. Make sure that there are only a few limits. Too many creates confusion. The limits that are set, however, need to be followed strictly.

Here are a few limits that help:

✓ build only as tall as you are (you do not want blocks falling on the children's heads)

✓ take out only those blocks you will be using

✓ blocks are only for building (point out how dangerous blocks can be if they are thrown or used for hitting)

✓ only knock down the building you built

✓ put away the blocks that you use

Note: This is not to discourage sharing, but to encourage personal responsibility. If a child is sharing the blocks with another child who wants to leave the Block Center, keep a clipboard and pencil handy for the exiting child to sign his name. Even if he cannot write, he will know his own mark. Remind him at clean up time to come back to help clean up.

Adding activities, and changing them frequently, renews the children's interest in the Center. Use only a few activities at a time. The main focus of the Center—the main material—is blocks. When you put other activities in the Center, make sure they are in a container like a basket, bucket or tray. Make sure that all of the necessary items to make the activity work are included in the container. Use rebuses to help give directions for the activity. This makes the work child-directed with the rebuses showing the children how to use the equipment properly.

Large Task Cards

3+

Language & Physical development

When children first use blocks for building, they may be a little overwhelmed by the task.

Materials

✓ construction paper
✓ markers
✓ tape

What to do

To help children get started, especially with three year olds and young fours, enlarge the task cards shown below, to the actual size of the blocks.

Place the enlarged cards in the Center for the children to build upon. (They actually place the blocks on top of the task card drawings).

When they are comfortable with this, tape the cards on the wall to which the children will refer as they construct. (At this point they will not place the blocks upon the task card drawing.)

When they have mastered this, put the task cards away. The children should be ready to construct and explore their block creations on their own.

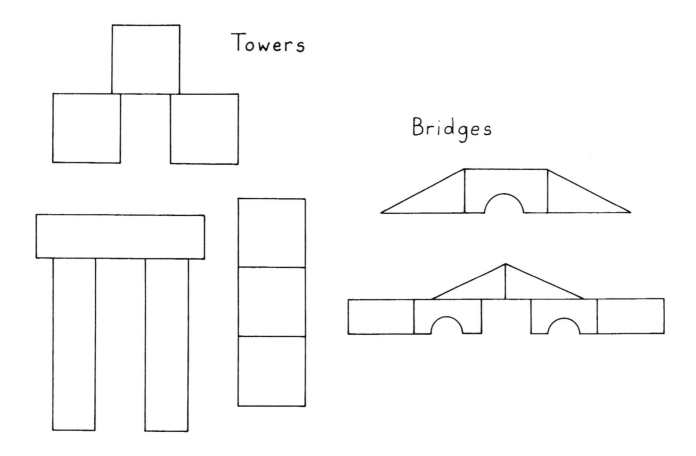

Towers

Bridges

Small Task Cards

To add a little challenge and variety, make small task cards for different themes.

Materials

✓ old magazines and books
✓ scissors
✓ construction paper
✓ glue
✓ large box

What to do

For example, if you are learning about doctors and hospitals, cut out pictures of hospitals, inside and outside scenes, from old magazines or books.

Glue these to sheets of construction paper.

Place them in a large box so the children can easily look through them, choose one and then try to build the picture with the blocks.

This can be done with any topic to broaden and to elaborate the children's experiences and learn throughout the curriculum.

Traffic Signs

Add traffic signs to the Block Center. You can buy them, but they can be made very easily, too.

Materials

✓ tagboard or index cards
✓ glue
✓ wooden construction toy, such as Tinkertoys®, or clay

What to do

Copy the signs below several times.

Cut out two signs for each traffic standard.

Glue them on both sides of tagboard or index cards, cut to the same shape as the signs on page 41.

To make the base, slip one end of a Tinkertoy® on the sign; insert the other into a Tinkertoy® joint for the base.

Use a piece of clay for the base if you need an alternative.

When children make the signs, they can have as many signs as they like with the variety they prefer.

Make a Sign

3+

Language development

Reading and writing can occur in the Block Center by adding paper, pencils and tape for the children to create a sign for their constructions; or, to write a message like, "Don't knock my building down" in invented spelling.

Materials

✓ different kinds of paper, in assorted shapes and sizes
✓ pencils, pens and markers
✓ container

What to do

Put the materials in the container and place in the Block Center.

The children use the materials to make signs or labels for their constructions whenever they wish.

This activity should be available for the children to use the entire year. Include additional reading and writing tools periodically.

Environmental Signs

3+

Physical development

Environmental signs are another way to encourage reading in the Block Center.

Materials

✓ scissors
✓ glue
✓ index cards
✓ self-adhesive paper
✓ tape
✓ container
✓ logos from local stores and businesses

What to do

To make the signs, collect logos of the stores in your neighborhood.

Cut out the logos and glue them to index cards. It is helpful to laminate the cards or to cover them with clear self-adhesive paper.

Place the cards and a roll of tape in a container and place the container in a designated spot on a shelf on which blocks are stored.

The children take out a sign and tape it to their constructions, labeling it.

Accessories

3+

Physical development

There are many low cost materials that can be added to the Block Center to enhance the block play.

Materials

assorted materials (see list below)

What to do

Put out one or two materials at a time.

Put them away when the children show that they have lost interest. This is a partial list of materials. (Many can be saved by the teacher or by the parents.)

✓ old candles with the wicks cut off
✓ pieces of sponge cut into a variety of shapes
✓ placemats that have scenes on them
✓ old toy pieces
✓ beanbags of different shapes
✓ old plastic flowers
✓ architectural magazines
✓ toy cars and trucks

✓ shiny paper (to be used to depict water)
✓ paper towel cylinders (to be used to construct tunnels)
✓ styrofoam peanuts (to be used to depict snow)
✓ packing material, like corners used to protect furniture (to depict roofs)
✓ egg-shaped stocking containers (used to depict domes)
✓ tile, linoleum scraps and indoor and outdoor carpet scraps

Paper People

3+

Physical development

Art

Wood block figures are a great addition to the Center. If you do not have any, make them.

Materials

✓ magazines
✓ tagboard
✓ self-adhesive paper
✓ tape

✓ scissors
✓ glue
✓ blocks

What to do

Find whole body pictures in magazines or in old books, or use paper dolls and cut them out.

Glue them to tagboard for stiffness and cut them out again. For longer use, cover them with clear self-adhesive paper or laminate them.

Tape each figure to a block so that it will stand up when the children use them. The neat thing about paper figures is that you can have enough for everyone; each child has a family to work with.

Make families to match those of the children.

Create paper vehicles of all kinds or characters that relate to the themes you use.

Seasonal Trees

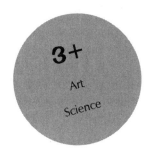

3+

Art

Science

To add trees to the Block Center, consider making them instead of buying them. They are easy to replace if they are damaged.

Materials (to make 6 trees)

✓ 6 twigs about 2'-3' long   ✓ large ball of clay
✓ liquid glue   ✓ hot glue gun (for teachers only)
✓ artificial leaves   ✓ plastic snow
✓ scissors   ✓ dish pan
✓ cotton balls or pieces of cotton

What to do

To make the leaves, cut numerous smaller leaves from the larger artificial ones.

Make six small balls of clay and push each twig into the clay ball. Flatten the clay ball so that it rests flat on the work table with the twig extending vertically from the top of the clay ball.

Use the hot glue gun to attach the fall leaves to two of the twigs, attach the green leaves to two other twigs.

Take the remaining two (plain) twigs and cover them with liquid glue.

Stick cotton balls or pieces of cotton on the twigs to resemble snow.

The children use the trees to enhance the buildings and houses they construct in the Block Center.

Dominoes

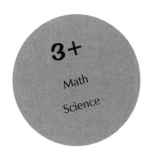

3+

Math

Science

Children enjoy seeing cause-and-effect that they initiate.

Materials

✓ rectangular blocks

What to do

Before the children arrive, stand the rectangular blocks upright in a straight line, about six inches apart.

When all of the children are in the Block Center to view the event, push the first block over.

Watch the results with the children.

Allow the children to rebuild the line and initiate the action again.

Talk about what happens.

When the children work in the Block Center, they will create the domino game over and over again, standing, transfixed, as the blocks tumble over.

Maze

3+

Language development

Math & Science

The Block Center is an excellent place to teach vocabulary words.

Materials

✓ blocks
✓ toy cars

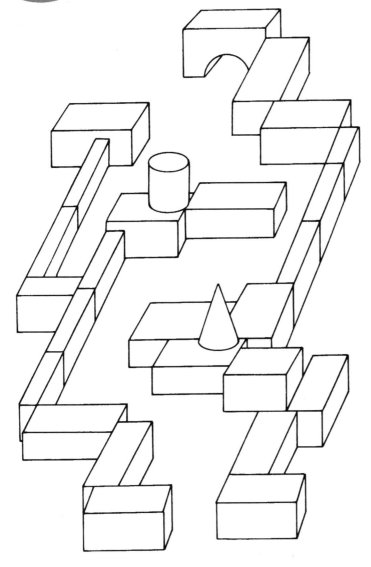

What to do

Most of the time, we want block play to be child-initiated. Occasionally the teacher needs to play a role in the play. Before the children arrive, build a maze with the blocks.

Have several toy cars available to use in the maze.

Introduce the maze to the children and discuss what the goal of a maze is, that is finding a way out.

The children use the teacher-created maze for several days.

When all of the children understand what the new word, "maze," means, the teacher moves aside and lets the children design their own mazes.

Obstacle Course

3+

Language
development

Math & Science

The obstacle course is another example of how the Block Center can be used for vocabulary building.

Materials

✓ blocks

What to do

As with the maze, the teacher builds the first obstacle course in the Center. It is introduced and it is used for a few days.

When the children have a clear understanding of what the words "obstacle course" means, they are encouraged to create their own.

Over the year it is amazing how elaborate the obstacle course becomes as the children use their imagination and their creativity.

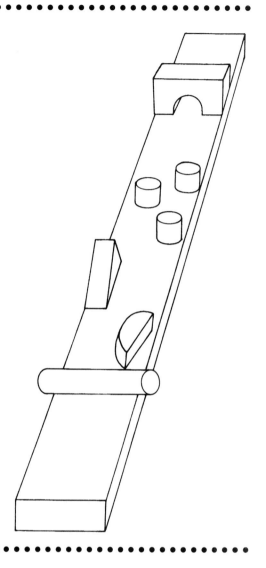

Three Little Pigs

3+

Language
development

Art

Literature does not have to be confined to the Library Center. It belongs in the Block Center, too, where blocks and props can tell a story over and over.

Materials

✓ tell or read *The Three Little Pigs*
✓ small bundle of hay
✓ twigs
✓ wooden blocks (covered in red paper or felt, if desired)
✓ large basket or container

What to do

After reading or telling *The Three Little Pigs* to the children, place *The Three Little Pigs* book and the props, in a large basket and display it in the Center.

The children will use the props to retell the story, completing the buildings described in the story with the props.

Try this with other stories using different props.

Build Within a Shape

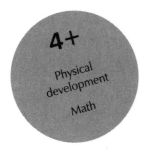

4+

Physical development

Math

Make block building more challenging by adding shape cards in which the children build their constructions.

Materials

✓ poster board
✓ markers
✓ clear self-adhesive paper or laminating film

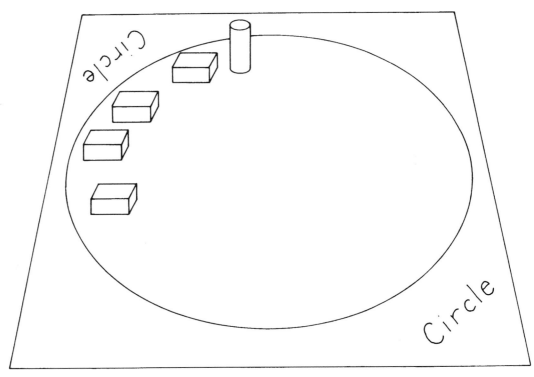

What to do

Use regular size poster board (about 28" x 22").

Make one shape on each piece of poster board. Draw different geometric shapes, like a circle, a square, a triangle, an oval and a diamond on the poster board pieces.

Make the shape slightly smaller than the poster board, to give the children lots of room to build.

Laminate each poster board piece for longer life.

The children choose a poster board with a shape and build a structure inside the shape.

Block Pattern Cards

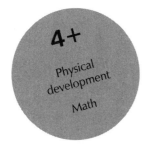

4+

Physical development

Math

Children can begin to make and recognize patterns with their block play.

Materials

✓ construction paper
✓ markers

What to do

Using the pattern card below as an example, make your own block pattern cards. Trace a variety of sequences on construction paper.

At first, make the pattern cards the size of the actual blocks. The children can then match the pattern by placing the correct block on top of the matching silhouette or shape, duplicating the pattern.

Later, they can match patterns when the shapes and silhouettes are not the actual size.

Learning to duplicate patterns is an important developmental skill for young children to acquire. Start with a simple, two block pattern and work toward three and four block patterns. Most of the children will enjoy the challenge of solving the pattern.

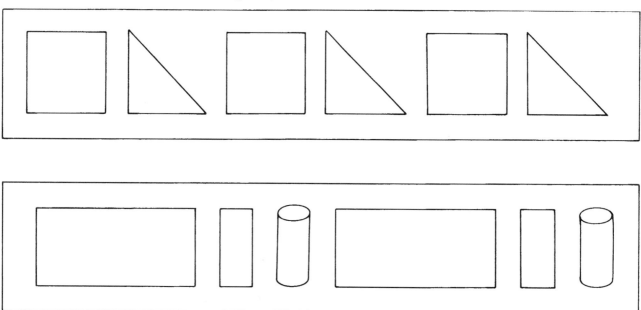

Part and Whole Relationship

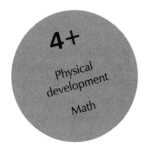

4+

Physical development

Math

To add another dimension to creating patterns, make a variety of block relationship pattern cards.

Materials

✓ construction paper
✓ markers

What to do

Use the example below for making your own cards.

At first, make the cards the actual size of the blocks. Later, make the cards smaller.

Since this activity is more difficult, but a very important developmental task for children, start with simple patterns and progress to the more difficult, as the children are ready.

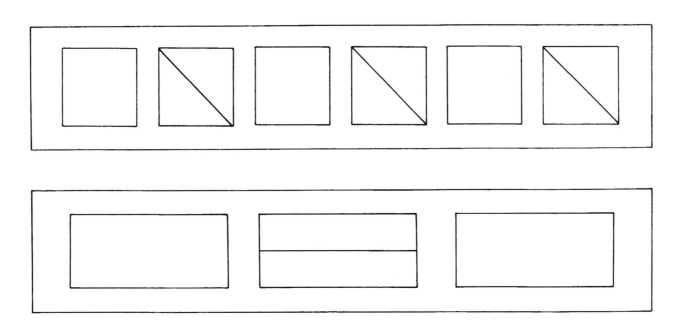

Floor Mat

4+

Physical
development

Math & Art

To begin developing the children's mapping skills, make a floor mat for the Block Center. Keep the design simple. The blocks themselves are the focus, so the floor mat needs to encourage block play.

Materials

✓ old white sheet   ✓ permanent markers

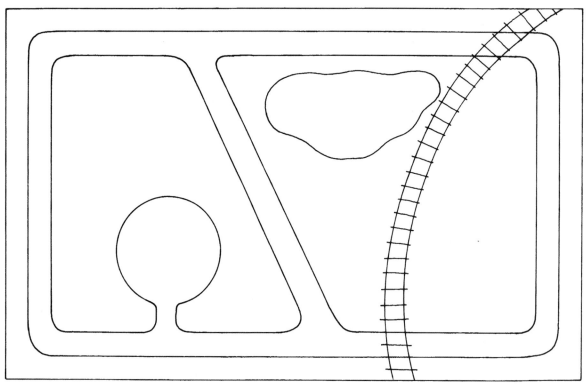

What to do

Many purchased mats are too busy, inviting children to use toy cars or trucks only. They run them around the streets on the mat because all of the buildings are already drawn in place.

Create a mat where the buildings need to be erected by the children using blocks.

On an old white sheet, with permanent markers, draw a simple road, leaving lots of open spaces for building homes, schools and retail stores (just like a good suburban planner).

Add a park with a lake and a railroad track. Remember, most of the mat needs to be free for block building.

Use the traffic signs described on page 40.

Measuring Tools

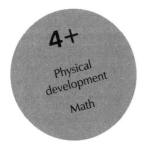

Having measuring tools available encourages the development of math skills.

Materials

✓ variety of measuring tools
✓ container

What to do

Collect a variety of measuring tools such as rulers, tape measures, yard sticks, fold out measuring sticks, unifix cubes and protractors and place them in the Center. This gives the children a choice of tools to use for measuring.

Eventually, the children will discover that measurement with each tool yields the same result (an inch measured with a ruler is an inch measured with a yardstick).

Place the measuring devices in a container and place the container in a designated spot, easily accessible to the children.

The children use the measuring devices as needed.

Nonstandard Measurers

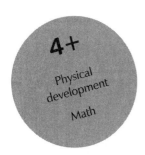

Before the children are ready to use yardsticks, rulers and the like, they may need practice using other items for measuring.

Materials

✓ variety of objects such as string, cut out feet, paper clip chain
✓ container

What to do

Have the children begin by using the blocks themselves. It is an excellent way to start.

When the children feel comfortable using the blocks, add other non-standard measuring objects. For example:

✓ add several lengths of string

✓ make a paper clip chain for measuring constructions

✓ make measurers by tracing around a child's foot or hand on poster board

✓ cut out ten of each tracing and place them in a basket

Objects like these are fun and they are excellent motivators for measuring structures. The children enjoy referring to a street outlined by the blocks as being "three of Kevin's feet long."

Parade Floats

4+

Social development

Art

Children love parades, but before they can organize parades in the Block Center, they must have an understanding of the word "float." To do this, add several teacher-made shoe box floats to the Center.

Materials

✓ shoe boxes
✓ assorted materials

What to do

Before school, the teacher builds a road with blocks and places the shoe box floats in the Center (the children will need to spend some time in the Center with you as you explain, illustrate and experiment with the floats).

When you feel they have grasped the meaning of the word "float," and how floats are part of parades (it may take several days), put away your shoe box float and take apart the block road.

Now the children are ready to make their own floats out of the blocks themselves.

Put a box of artificial flowers, ribbons, crepe paper streamers, pompoms, old plastic figures, a roll of masking tape and other material you may have available.

Encourage the children to tape the materials to the blocks. Have the children parade their creations on a road of their own design. If you want, add circus figures to the parade props. Make them, following the directions for Traffic Signs (see page 40) or Paper People (see page 43).

Put Away Cards

3+

Language & Social development

Clean up time is a difficult time for children. It is much more fun if they play their way through it by making a game of it.

Materials

✓ construction paper
✓ markers

What to do

Use the cards below as examples of how to make Put Away Cards. The children each draw a card to begin clean up.

Every child working in the Center must select at least one or more cards until the clean up task is done.

Put away 3 ☐s.

Put away 2 ☐s.

Put away 4 ☐s.

Put away 1 △.

Chapter 3

The Construction Center

The Construction Center is one of the children's favorite places. All the activities are open-ended. There is no right answer, no essential conclusion. The children play with plastic interlocking toys such as Legos®, wooden connecting toys such as Tinkertoys®, plastic connecting toys such as Bristle Blocks®, Unifix Cubes®, wooden logs sets, such as Lincoln Logs® and similar toys. They work for as long or as short a time as they like. Here the children explore the process of putting things together and taking things apart. They may or may not have a finished product, but finished products are not important. What is important is trying things out. They experiment, initiate, create and problem solve. While working in the Construction Center children learn creative thinking and how to solve problems, two critical developmental tasks.

By having open-ended materials, the children can develop the ability to take different approaches to solve problems. "What would happen if I...?" they ask themselves. "Where will this fit? How can I make this side the same as the other one? How can I make an open space here?"

Language Development

The same is true of reading. The children have to follow a simple sequence to work with any of the materials. Being able to sequence events is essential to the sequencing of letters that is required for reading. Task cards with the words identifying the pictures present opportunities for reading. Having paper and pencils available in the Center enables children to make labels, write directions, draw pictures and to create signs for their construction.

Math

Math learning also happens in the Construction Center. When the children create a pattern with Unifix Cubes®, for example, or count Lego® pieces for each child to share, they are learning math. When they are using any of the materials to measure constructions or objects, they are learning math. These are just a few examples of the way math happens in this Center.

Social Development

Social skills develop as the children work in this Center and use the materials. The materials used can be used by one child or several. Most of the time, however, two or three children attempt to work on one construction together. Here the children have to make decisions about how the materials can best be shared, and about how they can take turns with scarce pieces. The children choose the best way to negotiate and to reach compromises. Most importantly, the Center offers a chance—a time—to talk and talk and talk to each other about feelings, ideas, frustrations and about the construction project itself. By working in small groups the children learn teamwork as they work and talk with each other. They learn friendship, what it takes to be a friend and how to earn consideration by others.

Creating the Construction Center

What is the best way to create an effective, child-centered Construction Center? It isn't too difficult to lay out. Choose a place in the classroom that is noisy anyway. This Center will add to the din. Place a large piece of carpeting in the area to establish the boundaries of the work space. The carpet size depends on the number of children you want in the Center at one time. Plan for at least two children but three or four is better. If you do not have a piece of carpeting, used colored tape (on tile flooring) or hook-sided velcro (on carpeting) to mark the work space. Remove the tape every Friday and replace it on Monday (if it is left over a long period of time it will damage the floor or carpet). A small bookcase will store the materials for the center, and it will define one side of the Center.

Use one material at a time. It is best not to have Legos®, Tinkertoys® and Bristle Blocks® in the Center at the same time, so you'll need large quantities of the materials being used. If you choose, Legos, for example, put them in several easy-to-carry trays (baskets, dish pans or buckets). When the children work they get a tray of Legos® from the shelf, work with it and when they are finished, refill the tray and return it to the shelf. Although the Legos will get mixed, from one tray to another, each child in the center will have the responsibility of his own tray to refill at clean-up time. Use rebuses (step-by-step picture directions) as much as possible. They show the children how to use the various materials properly. These simply drawn pictures invite the children to "read" along and to work at their own pace. Many of the illustrations that accompany the activities in this book can easily be converted into rebuses by adding the written direction to the picture. Consider the ability level of the class when adding the words.

The children's behavior lets you know when it is time to change the materials in the Center. If you notice a lack of interest, it is time to change. After one materials is put away for awhile, bring it out at a later date. The children will be glad to see an "old friend" again, and they will have matured enough to find new and different things to do and new ways to build with it.

Plastic Connecting Blocks

3+

Physical & Social development

Some materials are easier for young children to use than others. If children are just beginning to explore putting materials together, plastic connecting blocks, such as Bristle Blocks®, are ideal for them because they are easy to manage and they will stick together with very little effort. They do not require a precise fit.

Materials

✓ plastic connecting blocks, such as Bristle Blocks®
✓ basket or container

What to do

Encourage one child to build a structure and then have a friend attempt to duplicate it.

The children can discuss how the structures are the same and how they differ. This is a challenge for young children.

Velcro and Styrofoam

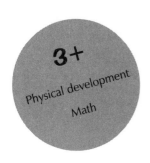

3+

Physical development

Math

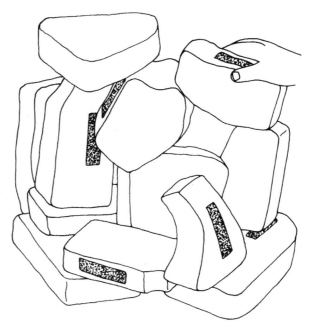

Children benefit from learning to conserve. A good way to conserve is to recycle. So recycle large, leftover pieces of styrofoam blocks for children's constructions.

Materials

✓ peel-and-stick velcro   ✓ large and small pieces of styrofoam

What to do

To make the construction blocks stick soft-side velcro on many of the flat surfaces and apply hook-side velcro on other flat block surfaces. Each type of velcro can go on the same block.

The children build by sticking the blocks together where the hook and the soft-side meet. They can build exciting constructions using the blocks. Their constructions will stay together and there is no precise fit.

When the blocks wear out, remove the velcro strips and hot glue them to other blocks.

Styrofoam Poke Construction

3+

Physical development

Puncturing styrofoam is another way to reuse styrofoam pieces. This activity can be done by an individual child or a group of children.

Materials

✓ large blocks of styrofoam
✓ colored toothpicks, twigs, golf tees, bamboo cooking skewers, artificial flowers, twist ties, popsicle sticks

What to do

Collect large blocks of styrofoam in any shape.

Collect golf tees, colored toothpicks, twigs, bamboo cooking skewers, artificial flowers, twist ties, drink stirrers, popsicle sticks and tongue depressors. For safety, snip off any sharp ends before allowing the children to use them.

The children use the materials to stick into the styrofoam blocks to create a construction.

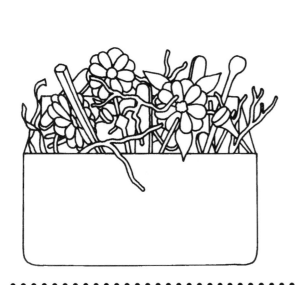

Nuts and Bolts Construction

3+

Physical development

Children develop fine motor skills when they use their small finger muscles to tighten and loosen nuts. Using different size nuts and bolts, also teaches children to match nuts to bolts; a matching skill related to recognizing similarities and differences.

Materials

✓ pegboard materials
✓ nuts and bolts

What to do

Collect small pieces of pegboard material. Often scrap pieces can be bought at a hardware store at a reasonable price.

Purchase matching nuts and bolts of varying sizes and lengths. Select bolts with a shaft that will pass through the pegboard holes.

Children attach the nuts and bolts to the pegboard, creating different designs.

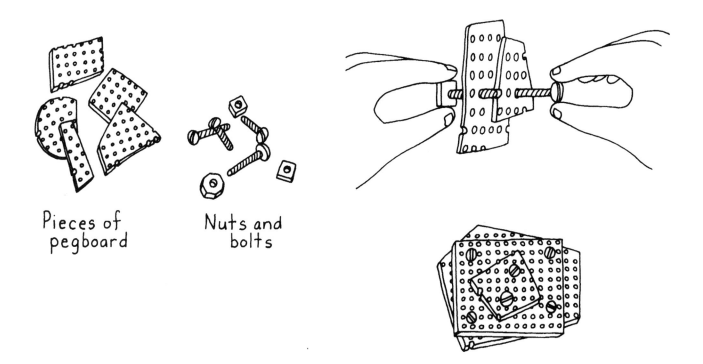

Pieces of
pegboard

Nuts and
bolts

Slotted Cardboard Construction

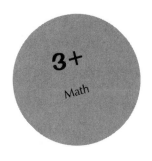

3+

Math

Recycle slotted cardboard inserts (found in boxes in which breakable items are shipped) to create an exciting, challenging construction activity.

Materials

✓ slotted cardboard inserts
✓ large box or tub
✓ plastic people or furniture (optional)

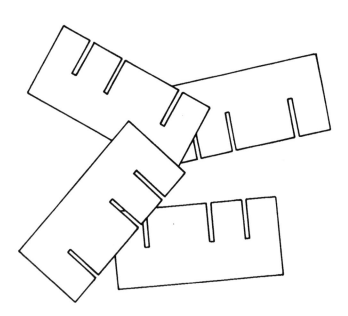
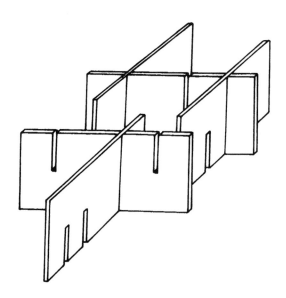

What to do

Collect a large number of slotted cardboard box inserts and place them in a large box or tub.

The children slip the cardboard together at the precut slots and build things tall and wide.

Add plastic people and furniture, and the children can create buildings and homes.

Interlocking Blocks

Interlocking blocks, such as Legos®, offer many opportunities to make different structures. They can work briefly and create a simple structure, or they can work for an extended time and build a complex one.

Materials

✓ plastic interlocking blocks
✓ construction paper
✓ markers

What to do

To help children challenge their building skills, duplicate the cards below.

Fill in the blanks with the number of blocks to be used. Have the children count the blocks and use them in their constructions.

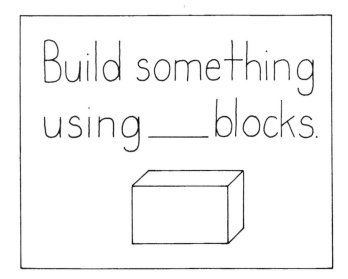

Color the picture on the card the color of the blocks the children should use. Then the card might say, "Build something using 10 blocks." The block on the card would be colored blue if you wanted the children to build with the blue blocks. Another card might say, "Build something using 25 blocks." The picture on the card would be colored yellow if you wanted the children to build with yellow blocks.

This is an excellent way to incorporate math and color recognition into the Construction Center.

Spools and Buttons

Creating patterns is an important skill in learning to read and in learning math. Using buttons and spools to make patterns is a good way to enhance these skills.

Materials

✓ empty thread spools
✓ large buttons

✓ spray paint (optional)
✓ long shoe strings in different colors

What to do

Collect empty thread spools from a seamstress or a dry cleaners that does alterations. If you are ambitious, these can be spray painted different colors.

Ask parents to save large buttons with large center holes (garage sales or flea markets are also good sources for buttons).

Purchase long shoe strings of different colors.

The children use the shoe string to thread the spools and buttons, randomly or with an established patterns.

Interlocking Block Task Cards

3+

Language development

Math

Often children need help getting started with their constructions. A good idea starter is to have construction task cards available. The task cards consist of real places, building, machines or other interesting places and things. Exposing the children to different architectural designs can inspire an interest in fine arts.

Materials

✓ scissors
✓ glue
✓ markers
✓ self-adhesive paper or laminating film
✓ shoe box or other container
✓ 5" x 8" or 4" x 6" colored index cards
✓ old magazines and books

What to do

Make building task cards on 5" x 8" or 4" x 6" colored index cards. Use old magazines or books as a resource for collecting colorful pictures of buildings, castles, bridges and vehicles like ships and trains.

Cut the picture to fit the index cards and glue to the cards.

Write on the bottom the words that best describe the picture.

Laminate or cover with clear self-adhesive paper so the task cards will last throughout many handlings over time.

Place the cards in a shoe box or other container. Place the box in the Construction Center so the children can chose a card to inspire their construction. They can use these task cards with any of the materials used in the Center, not just with the interlocking blocks.

Wooden Connecting Toys

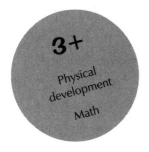

3+

Physical development

Math

Wooden connecting toys, such as Tinkertoys®, are interesting and offer a different type of material for constructing. With the long sticks and round bases, the children have a different building experience.

Materials

✓ shallow container
✓ construction paper
✓ clear self-adhesive paper or laminating film
✓ wooden connecting toys, such as Tinkertoys®

✓ stop watch
✓ markers

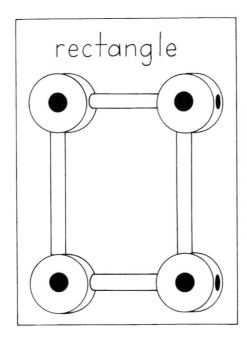

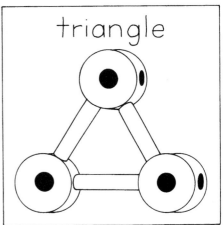

What to do

To keep the toys from being dumped by the children on the floor (to find just the right piece), place them in a shallow container like a low-sided dish pan or tote tray.

The children take the container from the shelf, build with the toys and return the container to the shelf when they are finished.

To engage and challenge their construction skills, duplicate, color and back the cards below with construction paper.

Cover them with clear self-adhesive paper or laminate to preserve them. If the activities illustrated prove to be too simple a task for the children, use a stop watch to time their speed in making each shape or a group of shapes.

Challenge them to create other geometric shapes. Create cards with the new shapes.

Three-Dimensional Shapes

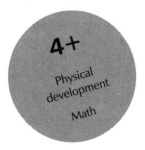

4+

Physical development

Math

Another challenge with wooden connecting toys, such as Tinkertoys®, is to make three dimensional shapes by adding on or piggy-backing one shape on the next. Encourage them to think of how many times they can make one of the geometric shapes then duplicate it, attaching it to the first.

Materials

✓ wooden connecting toys, such as Tinkertoys®
✓ construction paper
✓ markers
✓ clear self-adhesive paper or laminate

What to do

Challenge older children to make one diamond (like the one on the card), then make a second and attach it to the first; the third is made and attached to the second; and the fourth diamond is made and attached to the first, the second and the third.

In this activity the children would only have to make sure that each diamond addition is attached to any of the diamonds. In other words, sides can be shared by two diamonds.

They continue this until there are no more ways to add a diamond to the construction.

Try this activity with other shapes.

Wooden Log Sets

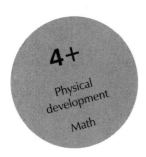

4+

Physical development

Math

Wooden log sets, such as Lincoln Logs®, are a bit more difficult to use than some of the other construction materials. It is best to save them for later in the year when the children have developed more fine motor skills and a longer attention span. To develop a construction with this material takes time and focus.

Materials

✓ scissors
✓ glue
✓ tape
✓ wooden log set(s), such as Lincoln Logs®
✓ local newspapers and advertisements, store containers
✓ clear self-adhesive paper or laminating film

✓ index cards
✓ box

What to do

Make signs for the children to attach to their constructions.

Cut out local store logos from the newspaper or from store containers or wrappings.

Glue the logos to index cards (4" x 6") and cover them with clear self-adhesive paper or laminate the cards.

Place the cards in a box along with a roll of clear tape. The children use the cards by taping them to their construction, creating a local familiar store.

Cubes, Cubes

All ages enjoy using Unifix Cubes®. Not only are they good for developing fine motor skills but they can also be used to develop math and reading skills. Until children can understand patterning they will not understand word patterns or see the patterns in numbers.

Materials

✓ unifix cubes
✓ markers
✓ glue
✓ box or container

✓ index cards
✓ construction paper
✓ clear self-adhesive paper or laminating film

What to do

One way to use the cubes is to create color patterns with them. To get the children started creating patterns, make pattern cards and color them several different two-sequence patterns (such as red, green, red, green).

Also make several three-sequence pattern cards. After coloring the pattern cards, glue to construction paper. It is best to laminate them or cover them with clear self-adhesive paper.

Place the cards in a box or container. The children choose a card from the box and use the cubes to duplicate the pattern. After the children have explored the pattern cards for awhile, put them away. This will encourage them to create their own patterns.

Measuring

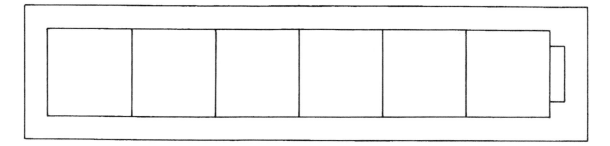

To develop math skills further, use the Unifix Cubes® for measuring.

Materials

✓ Unifix Cubes®   ✓ pencil and paper

What to do

Have the children create a long row of Unifix Cubes®.

Each child lays down beside the row of connected cubes.

Another child, the measurer, removes the cubes that go past the child's feet.

Then, together, they count the cubes from head to toe and record the information on the sheet of paper.

Each child's height is measured and recorded.

The children then can compare each person's height by looking at the recordings or making a class graph.

On another day, do the same activity with a tape measure and compare it to the Unifix Cube® results.

Paper Clip Measuring

Objects can be measured in many ways. Nonstandard materials can be used just as effectively as a ruler and often the children are less resistant and more enthusiastic using these unique measuring materials. Measuring with a paper clip chain, for example, offers a chance for the children not only to measure, but the chance to make the measuring tool they will be using.

Materials

✓ colored paper clips   ✓ large basket

What to do

Place colored paper clips in a large basket. The clips can be all the same or different sizes.

Encourage children to make a chain as long as they can, then use the pictures below as a guide to show them how to measure objects and distances in the classroom.

You will find that children will go back frequently to add to their chain to measure greater distances and larger objects. They seem to want to correct their inaccurate predictions and find out the accuracy of their new estimates.

Paper Clip Construction

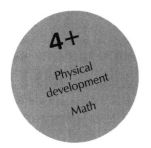

4+

Physical development

Math

Paper clips can be used as a construction tool as well as a measuring tool.

Materials

✓ paper clips   ✓ basket

What to do

The children can attach the clips randomly, side-to-side, end-to-end, end-to-side. They can begin from right-to-left or the reverse. For children who need a challenge, ask them to create certain shapes, then see how many ways they can make their construction.

Encourage the children to compare their constructions with each other to see the similarities and differences.

Parquetry Blocks

4+

Language development

Math

Parquetry blocks are an exciting and fun material to use in the Construction Center.

Materials

✓ parquetry blocks   ✓ paper
✓ peeled crayons   ✓ tray (optional)

What to do

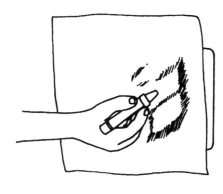
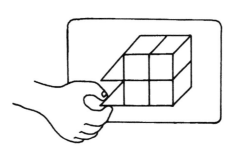

The children use the parquetry blocks to create all kinds of designs and patterns. Math skills are developed when children use these shapes to create designs. They design patterns, observe symmetry and develop figure ground perception.

Children can also make a picture of their designs. Provide sheets of paper and peeled crayons. When the children have created a design, they place a sheet of paper on top of it.

They use the side of the crayon to rub back and forth on the paper over the block design. The designs created by the children will appear on the paper. It is easier if they work on a tray so when they rub over it the pieces do not move.

Pipes

Keep children excited about and interested in the Construction Center by changing materials when they lose interest in a particular material. Plastic pipe pieces and connectors are a fun addition.

Materials

✓ plastic pipe pieces and connectors
✓ duct tape

What to do

Collect pieces of plastic pipe and connectors from parents or plumbers, or purchase them.

The trick to making pipe construction a success is to have lots of T and L connectors.

Also it helps to cut the pipes into manageable lengths. Cover any sharp edges with duct tape.

Challenge the children to create a system of pipes and connections that extends out from their bodies and comes back to them.

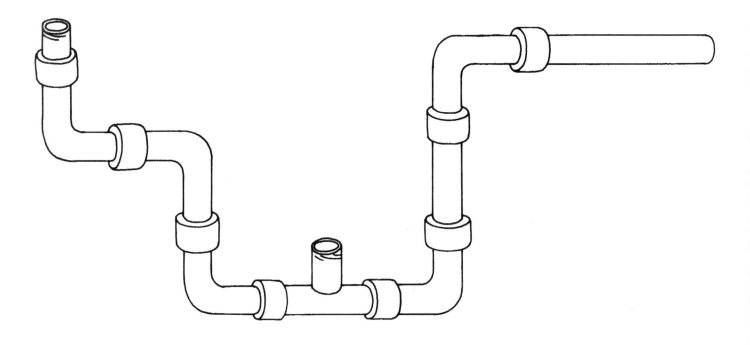

Floor Mat

4+

Language development

Math

To give the Construction Center a new look add a floor mat to be used with any of the materials and activities in this section. This will encourage the children to use the materials in a different way.

Materials

✓ old sheet or large piece of material
✓ scissors
✓ permanent markers

What to do

Cut the sheet to fit the area to be used in the center.

Use the markers to draw a very simple design on the sheet, leaving plenty of in-between spaces for the children's buildings.

The design can be a street plan, a room plan or a playground plan—any area of interest to the children.

By letting the children help design the mat, you have the perfect opportunity to introduce mapping skills. You can even make the mat relate to a theme on community helpers: post office, doctor's office, grocery store or fire station.

Parallel Play

5+

Social & Physical development

Sometimes children grow tired of using a material. This often happens when you are not ready to change it. Renew interest in the material by teaching the children a game to play. It can be done with any of the materials used in the Construction Center.

Materials

✓ construction center materials

What to do

Give two or three children the same amount of material.

Have the children sit with their backs to each other so they cannot see what the others are constructing.

When the children are finished using all their pieces, have them look at each other's constructions. They will be amazed at the different constructions they have created.

You can challenge them even further by having them sit back-to-back and asking one child to tell the other how he is building with the materials.

Encourage the child following the instructions to build the same object using just the other child's directions. Have the children take turns listening and following. This is an excellent way to encourage listening skills.

Clean-Up Activity

Clean up is a difficult time for children. It is always easier to get the materials out than it is to put them away. Make it fun by adding clean-up cards to the center.

Materials

✓ paper
✓ markers

What to do

Using put away cards makes clean up a game. While they are busy playing the game they are also working on counting and getting the job done.

Use the illustrations below as a model. They can be used with any materials of the same color in the Construction Center.

Make several cards like the ones below. Write in the number of items to be picked up and color the space the same color as the material to be picked up.

As the children develop their counting skills, challenge them by making new cards with larger numbers on them.

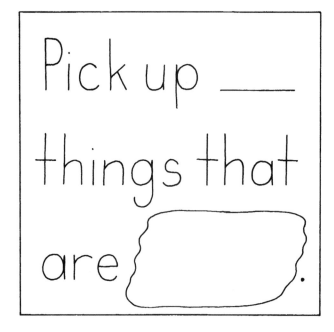

Chapter 4

The Dramatic Play Center

"Play like I'm the Mom and you're the Daddy, and Grandma is coming to visit," David said. "Play like you are sick and I am the doctor," said Lei. Children love to pretend. They love to take on adult roles, especially of family members and of people they know. The Dramatic Play Center is a place where children can assume the roles of the significant people in their lives. Some teachers call it the Homeliving Center, the Housekeeping Center or the Home Center. By whatever name, it is a place for children to experiment with adult roles, responsibilities and personalities. They also learn to work together and to problem solve in a familiar and comfortable place. They will choose this Center more often because of its homey, familiar feeling, spending hours playing and learning. What can be learned in the Dramatic Play Center? How can the environment be prepared to teach what we want children to learn? Discussed below is how the activities maximize learning.

Language Development: Reading and Writing

Carefully choose the materials in the Dramatic Play Center to create a place for reading and writing to happen in a natural way. Collect a variety of books that would normally be found in the home, like a dictionary, a cookbook, a telephone book, a magazine and other books that give illustrated directions (like a home repair book). Have writing tools and paper available for making notes beside the phone. Have blank recipe cards, numbered shopping list pads and stationary and envelopes. Create a bulletin board in the Center. Put a calendar, relevant photos, a phone list of the children in the class, a letter to the class, a resealable bag with shopping coupons and a numbered, must do list in the Center. All of these create reasons for the children to interact with print. Along with the various materials in the Center, place rebuses (picture direction cards) with activities and materials, showing the children how to use them properly. Reading the rebus teaches children to look for written instructions first and decide if they have enough to proceed on their own.

Language Development: Speaking and Listening

The variety of props and activities in the Dramatic Play Center give the children things to talk about and provide a constructive reason to talk. Language develops as children share their ideas while they play. Children learn new words when they talk about new props and materials.

Math

Children develop many math skills while playing in the Dramatic Play Center. When they put one glass with one plate on one placemat they are practicing one-to-one correspondence. When they put four pieces of pizza together to make one whole pizza, they are working on part/whole relationships, fractions in action. When they read their friends telephone numbers or dial the telephone to call friends, they are learning number recognition. When they count the numbers on the calendar or use the shopping list pad with numbers in numerical order, they are using number sequence. Putting fruits and vegetables in separate piles teaches children to classify. Math is part of most of the play that occurs in the Dramatic Play Center daily in an enjoyable and meaningful way.

Physical Development

Children develop fine motor skills when they put on dress-up clothes. They must button, zip, hook and snap clothes to get into them—great for their little fingers and hands. When they dial the phone, write a must do list or fill the baby bottle they are using small muscles necessary for writing. When they wash the baby, cook, wash the dishes or make the bed, the larger muscle groups come into play. When they are crawling, rolling, jumping and hopping, pretending to be animals, muscle development occurs naturally, comfortably and enthusiastically.

Social Development

Children pass through predictable social development stages that are observable in the Dramatic Play Center. The first stage is the unoccupied, spectator stage, where the children wander around, looking and watching. The next stage is the onlooker stage where the children watch others, ask questions and make suggestions, but they do not participate in the play. The next stage is solitary play where children select toys with which to play, but they are not interested in what other children are doing. Parallel play is the next stage, where a child plays near another child, playing with the same object, but not interacting. Associative play, the next stage, is where the child plays with others, engaging in the activities, excluding some children, but rarely negotiating the direction of their play. The last stage is cooperative play where the children organize their play, assigning roles and negotiating terms and turns. If children have had few social opportunities earlier, they will start at the spectator stage (regardless of their age) and pass through the first few stages rapidly. Observing children and understanding their play, helps you select toys, props and materials to include in the Center. It also helps you to select the appropriate materials—suitable to the developmental level of the children. In the Dramatic Play Center children make choices, decisions and take on leadership and fellowship roles. They discover socially acceptable behavior and they learn skills appropriate to group behavior.

Social Studies

As children explore in basic family routines in the Dramatic Play Center they develop the concept of the roles of family members. They discover ways of helping each other. By having a variety of tools, props, baby dolls and clothing, children can learn to appreciate and celebrate different cultures. When the Dramatic Play Center is a fire station, a veterinarian's office, a florist shop or a grocery store, children are also be able to identify some basic economic needs. They also take on the roles of these community members and they learn about their jobs.

Creating the Dramatic Play Center

A Dramatic Play Center that meets the needs of the children, created for learning, in a warm and comfortable setting can happen with planning. Here are some things to consider. Because space is often a limiting factor, try to locate the Center out of the traffic pattern. It can be a noisy place, so locate it with the other noisy centers. Have clearly defined boundaries. Try putting it in the corner of the room. That will give you two boundaries; position the Center furniture to provide the other two. Boundaries say to the children, "This is where these materials belong." Leave a small entry into the Center to discourage the children from taking materials elsewhere.

It is helpful to divide the Dramatic Play Center into two areas—the kitchen and the bedroom—if you have the space. Eating and sleeping are central to young children's lives, so giving them opportunities to play out these situations is essential. Provide a child-size sink, a stove, a refrigerator, a hutch or a cabinet for dishes and a table and chair. You can add an ironing board and a high chair if you have space. Cut down the handle of adult-size mops and brooms and add them to the Center. A small whisk broom and dust pan can be added, also. On each piece of furniture, put a picture label showing the child what goes in each furniture piece. For instance, if you store the pots and pans under the sink, draw pots and pans on an index card and attach it to the sink. This is a constant reminder to the children to return the pots and pans to under the sink. Provide pots and pans, unbreakable dishes and flatware, plastic fruits and vegetables and other pretend food items (they can be purchased wherever pet supplies are sold), empty cans opened at the bottom, empty food boxes and other containers. All of these items help the children act out the different family roles.

In the bedroom area, it is ideal to have a bed large enough for a child to get in. A bureau drawer with a large pillow or a crib mattress works well. If you have a doll bed, but no other bed the children can lay in, they may attempt to lie down in the doll bed and may break it. Have a bedside table, a sturdy child-size rocking chair and low open shelving. Collect several laundry baskets to fit on the shelving. In one basket, put shoes and boots; in another, purses and hats; in another, dresses; in another, coats and ties; and in another put baby things. On each basket, put a picture label showing the children what goes in each basket. That way, clean up time is well organized and clear. Be sure to put story books on the bedside table, to read before bedtime. Encouraging reading in the home is very important.

Keep the Dramatic Play Center a home center for eight to ten weeks; or, for as long as the children's interest level remains high. The children need lots of time, at first, to try out different domestic roles. When you feel the children are ready, change the Center to something familiar to them like a pet shop or grocery store. Later, move to more unfamiliar settings, like the Veterinarian's office or a fruit and vegetable stand. As the year evolves, have the children take a greater part in deciding how to change the Center. At first, let them help you put away a previous setting or theme. Next, let them help you put out the materials needed for a new setting or theme. Have them be in charge of making the decisions about where each object is placed. The older children can make picture identification signs and help draw rebus direction cards. The final step is to have the children create the whole center. They can brainstorm what could be in the Center and plan where it will go. They then bring props or make them for the new theme. The Center becomes theirs. Your role has evolved to that of a resource person. It is gratifying and exciting when children can create, manage, organize and maintain the center by themselves.

The themes used in the Center work best when you start with the familiar and work over time toward the less known. Home, pets, grocery store, bakery are more familiar concepts than circus, space or florist, for example. Always remember to include centers that are meaningful to the children. The same idea applies to the basic props. The boxes and cans you make available at first should be familiar items like dry cereal, animal crackers and string bean and tuna cans. Later on, introduce less familiar items to them, like beet cans and rice cake boxes. Other props, like a clothes iron, work best when they are the real thing. Flea markets are a good source for non-working appliances and they are fairly inexpensive (be sure to cut off all of the electrical cords on these appliances). Later, the children can move to the more abstract props like a wooden representation of a clothes iron.

This chapter is filled with exciting, easy-to-make props for children to use in the Dramatic Play Center. Let the children help as much as possible with the creation of these props. They will enjoy playing with the props even more if they are involved in making them.

With careful planning and thought the Dramatic Play Center can become a rich learning environment, inviting children to expand their knowledge and skills about the everyday world in which they live.

Picture Identification Cards

3+

Language & Social development

Picture Identification Cards help the organization of the Center by showing the children where items belong.

Materials

✓ 4" x 6" index cards
✓ glue
✓ scissors
✓ clear self-adhesive paper

What to do

Draw the cards necessary for your Dramatic Play Center (or use pictures from school supply catalogs).

Color each card, glue them to an index card and cover with clear self-adhesive paper.

Tape the cards to the bookcase or storage area where the items belong.

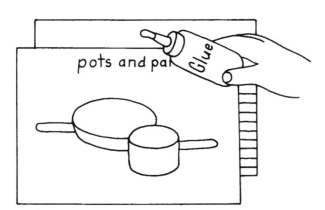

Color each card.

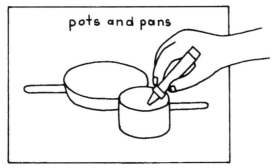

Glue card to index card.

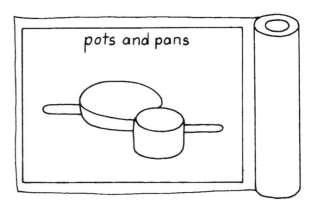

Cover with clear contact paper.

Role Card

3+

Physical & Social development

The following Role Cards are best used at the beginning of the year to help a child select a role and act it out. When children get used to acting out roles, change the cards, adding ones that require more thought and imagination.

Materials

✓ magazines
✓ yarn
✓ scissors

✓ 4" x 6" index cards
✓ hole punch
✓ glue

Glue magazine picture to index card.

Thread yarn through holes at the top of the card.

What to do

Cut a picture of a person, such as a mother or story book character from the magazines.

Glue it to the index card.

Punch two holes at the top of the card.

Cut 24" of yarn and thread it through the two holes. Tie it off.

A child puts on the necklace and pretends to be the character in the picture.

Other necklaces you could make are Daddy, Grandma, Grandpa, dog, cat, sister, brother, baby and any of the community workers.

Car

3+

Physical development

Social Studies

One of these cars will not be enough.*

Materials

✓ cardboard box, approximately 9" x 9" x 18"
✓ red, yellow, black and white construction paper
✓ glue
✓ thick yarn
✓ scissors

What to do

Cut out a large rectangle from the bottom of the box.

Cut out an oval from the top of the box.

Make holes in the front and back sides of the box.

Tie the yarn from the front hole to the rear hole on both sides of the box.

Cut out four black circles, 5" in diameter and glue them on the sides of the box.

Cut out two red ovals about 3" x 2" and glue them on the back of the box.

Cut out two yellow circles 2" in diameter and glue them on the front of the box.

Cut out semicircles and draw on dials (for the dashboard of the car) and glue them on the front of the box.

A child can wear the car and drive it on the road.

Cut out an oval from top of box. Make small holes in each corner.

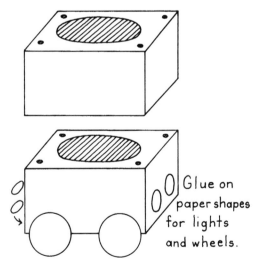

Glue on paper shapes for lights and wheels.

Create straps with yarn.

dials

To make "dashboard", draw dials onto cut out semi-circles and glue to front of box top.

*With this prop and all other Dramatic Play props described in this chapter, involve the children in making the prop.

Gas Pump

3+

Physical development

Social Studies

This prop fits into a transportation or machines theme.

Materials

✓ 1 or 2 boxes glued together to measure approximately 24″ x 12″ x 12″
✓ aluminum foil   ✓ glue
✓ 3′ length of garden hose   ✓ long nail
✓ piece of cork   ✓ 18″ x 18″ piece of cardboard
✓ white paper   ✓ scissors

What to do

Make a hole in the side of the box at the top; insert the hose.

Reach inside the box and push the nail through the hose; push the cork on the nail point.

Tape the box closed.

Glue cardboard on the box.

Cover the box with aluminum foil.

Cut white paper into a rectangle (for the price and gallon sign) and glue it on the box.

Place in the Dramatic Play Center. (But don't be surprised if it gets used throughout the classroom, even outside.)

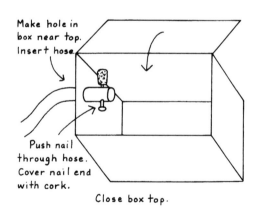

Make hole in box near top. Insert hose.

Push nail through hose. Cover nail end with cork.

Close box top.

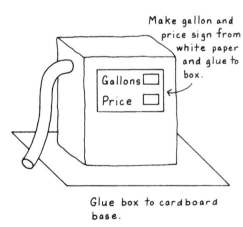

Make gallon and price sign from white paper and glue to box.

Gallons

Price

Glue box to cardboard base.

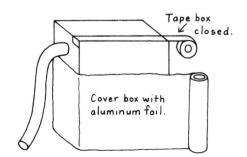

Tape box closed.

Cover box with aluminum foil.

Horse

3+

Language & Physical development

A horse is an indispensable prop in the Dramatic Play Center.

Materials

✓ empty, colored, liquid detergent bottle (without a handle and label)
✓ different colors of felt pieces
✓ glue
✓ long piece of ribbon
✓ broom stick
✓ hot glue gun

What to do

Cut a hole, the size of the broom handle in the side of the detergent bottle, toward the rear of the bottle.

Cut a mane out of felt and glue it on the bottle.

Cut eyes out of felt and glue them on the bottle.

Cut a forelock out of felt and glue it on the bottle.

Cut ears out of felt and glue them on.

Tie a ribbon around the bottle top.

Apply hot glue with the glue gun on the end of the broom handle and push the broom handle into the hole on the bottle.

Place in the Dramatic Play Center.

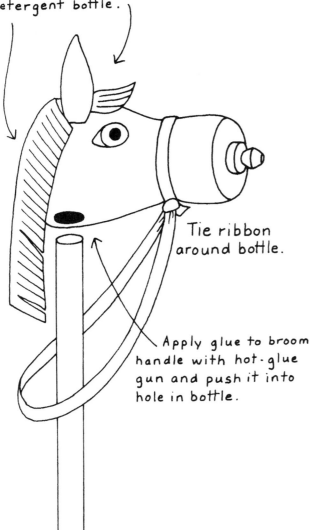

Cut eyes, ears, mane and forelock from felt and glue to detergent bottle.

Tie ribbon around bottle.

Apply glue to broom handle with hot-glue gun and push it into hole in bottle.

Dog Ears

3+

Language & Physical development

This prop fits into a pet or animal theme. Depending on the materials used (like the size of the shoulder pads, for example), you can create many types of animals. The example below shows how to make dog ears.

Materials

✓ head band
✓ 2 shoulder pads
✓ scissors
✓ hot glue gun

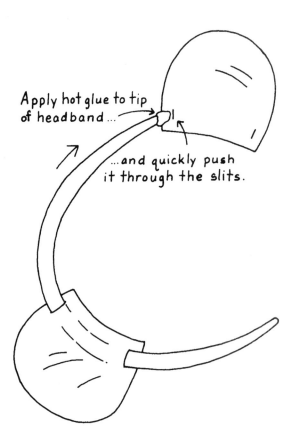

Apply hot glue to tip of headband...

...and quickly push it through the slits.

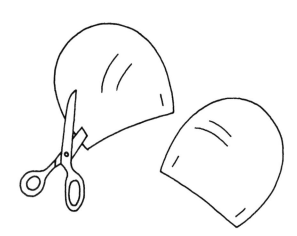

Cut a slit into each corner of two shoulder pads.

What to do

Cut a slit in each side of the shoulder pads.

Apply hot glue to the head band and quickly push it through one of the headband slits, holding it firmly.

Repeat the above step for the other shoulder pad.

Place in the Dramatic Play Center so a child can pretend to be a dog.

Starch Hat

3+

Physical development

Social Studies

This hat can be used with any theme where a child needs a hat. Although a spring hat is the example, it can be shaped into any hat style. Children love to help make these hats.

Materials

✓ several large mixing bowls, buckets or flower pots (the bowl is used as the mold that shapes the hat so any interesting container that fits a child's head works great)

✓ large pan   ✓ liquid starch
✓ artificial flowers   ✓ glue
✓ scissors   ✓ small bits and pieces of ribbon

✓ 2 large pieces of butcher paper cut into circles, 24" in diameter (any color) for each child making a hat.

What to do

Pour the starch into the large pan. Hold the paper circles together and dip them in the liquid starch until they are dripping.

Turn the mixing bowl (or other container) upside down and place the wet paper over it.

When the hat is dry, decorate it with flowers and ribbon bits.

Place in the Dramatic Play Center.

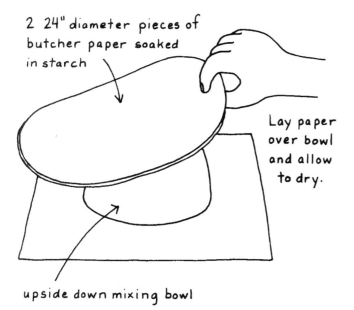

2 24" diameter pieces of butcher paper soaked in starch

Lay paper over bowl and allow to dry.

upside down mixing bowl

Remove hat from mold and decorate with flowers and ribbon bits.

Stocking Masks

3+

Language development

Social Studies

Stocking Masks can be used with any theme. They work especially well with animals or with storybook characters. After children learn how to make and use masks, they can make them at any time. You can make any kind, any animal or character you can imagine. The example below is a bear face, but adapt it to make any mask. One advantage of making this kind of mask is that children can see through them, and they do not have to put them on.

Materials

- ✓ coat hangers
- ✓ black yarn
- ✓ scissors
- ✓ glue

- ✓ clean, discarded stockings (any color)
- ✓ brown yarn
- ✓ masking tape
- ✓ brown, black, red and white felt

What to do

Bend the coat hanger into a circular shape and cover with the stocking.

Tie the stocking at the top, cut off the excess and tape around the bottom.

Fold the hook end closed and tape around it.

Cut ears from the brown felt; glue on the top of the mask.

Cut twelve pieces of brown yarn, each about 4" long, and glue them to the top of the mask.

Make the eyes. Cut two ovals from black felt, two smaller circles from white felt and glue them on the mask.

Make the nose. Cut a heart shape from red felt and glue it on the mask.

Cut two 6"-8" pieces of black yarn and glue them to the mask.

Place in the Dramatic Play Center.

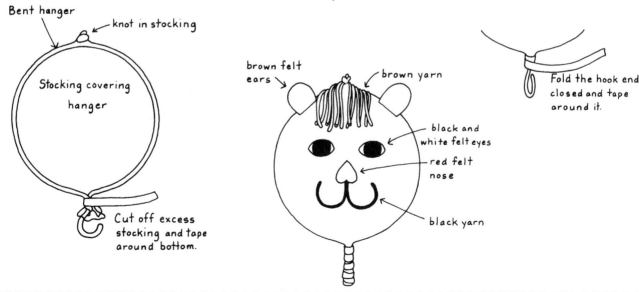

Bent hanger

knot in stocking

Stocking covering hanger

Cut off excess stocking and tape around bottom.

brown felt ears

brown yarn

black and white felt eyes

red felt nose

black yarn

Fold the hook end closed and tape around it.

Goggles

3+

Language development

Social Studies

Children love to use Goggles any time, but especially during a theme of frogs, scuba divers, beach play, colors or sports. The example below is a frog mask, but change it as needed, use any color, even make bifocals.

Materials

✓ ring from a 6-pack
✓ green cellophane
✓ scissors
✓ black marker

✓ elastic thread
✓ large-eye needle (like a darning needle)
✓ access to a laminating machine

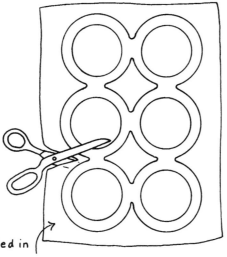

Six-pack rings laminated in green cellophane
Cut apart in pairs and trim off excess cellophane.

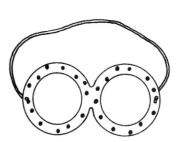

Attach elastic thread headband. Apply black dots to frame.

What to do

Cut the green cellophane to a size slightly larger than the size of the 6-pack ring. Place the 6-pack ring with the cellophane over it through the laminating machine.

Cut the rings part into pairs.(You will have three pairs.)

Thread the needle with the elastic thread and make a headband to hold the goggles on the children's heads.

Put black dots all around the frame of the goggles.

Place the goggles in the Dramatic Play Center and watch the children use their imagination.

Note: Make goggles without cellophane for a scuba diver, with purple cellophane for sun goggles, yellow for snow goggles, or make a set of the primary colors for the children to see their world through that color. One pair of goggles can be placed over another pair (essentially, "mixing" them) on the child's face, experimenting with primary colors.

Pizza

3+

Language & Physical development

Social Studies

Make pizzas with the children while focusing on a theme of foods, homeliving or restaurants.

Materials

✓ felt (red, green, light brown, white, orange and yellow)
✓ scissors   ✓ glue
✓ resealable bags   ✓ cardboard pizza circles
✓ pizza box, sized to the pizza

What to do

Set one pizza circle aside (it will be the pizza base).

Cut the brown felt to fit the second circle, forming the crust. Glue the felt to the cardboard.

Cut the felt-covered, cardboard circle into four pieces. Put the pieces in a plastic resealable bag.

Cut tomato sauce from red felt for each of the four pizza slices. Put the pieces in a plastic resealable bag.

Cut mushrooms from brown felt. Put the pieces in a resealable bag.

Cut onion from white felt. Put the pieces in a resealable bag.

Cut pepperoni from orange felt. Put the pieces in a resealable bag.

Cut bell peppers from green felt. Put the pieces in a resealable bag.

Cut olives from green and red felt. Put the pieces in a resealable bag.

Cut cheese from yellow felt. Put the pieces in a resealable bag.

A child creates a pizza using the pieces.

Keep in a pizza box.

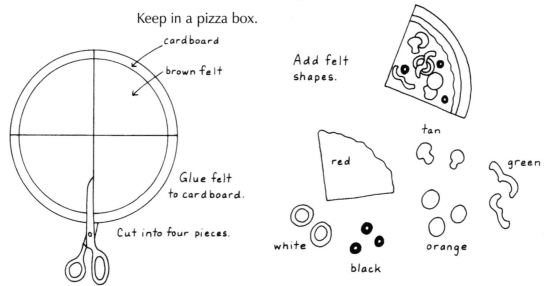

Stocking Food

3+

Language development

Social Studies

Children will enjoy making and using these props for a food, farm, grocery store or basic home living theme.

Materials

✓ clean, used stockings: one white, one brown
✓ small rubber bands
✓ dry-cleaning plastic bags
✓ black marker

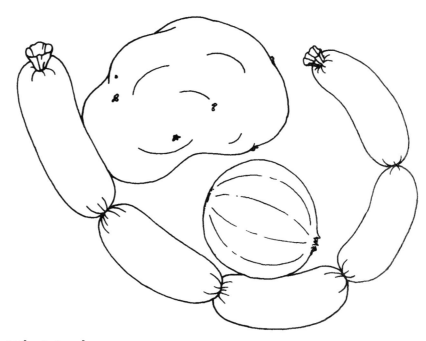

What to do

To make a potato, stuff the stocking foot with several dry-cleaning bags, 4″ to 5″ into the stocking. To close the potato, wrap a rubber band around the open end. Make black spots on the stocking for the potato eyes.

To make an onion, stuff dry-cleaning bags 2″ to 3″ into the white stocking. To close the onion, put a rubber band around the open end.

To make a sausage, stuff the stocking with dry-cleaning bags 6″ into the stocking. Tie off the open end with a rubber band and apply additional rubber bands every 2″ down the length of the sausage (making sausage links).

A child can go shopping for groceries.

Scale

3+

Social Studies

Math

A scale is invaluable in the Dramatic Play Center.

Materials

✓ cardboard pizza circle   ✓ aluminum cake pan
✓ string   ✓ scissors
✓ glue   ✓ hole punch
✓ marker   ✓ brass fasteners
✓ small piece of red poster board

What to do

Write the numerals 0 to 10 around the pizza circle.

Make an arrow from the red poster board. Use a brass fastener to attach it to the middle of the circle.

Punch three, evenly spaced holes around the cake pan.

Punch a hole at the bottom of the pizza circle.

Tie three strings in the holes of the cake pan.

Tie the strings in the hole on the pizza circle.

A child can pretend to weigh food (and other items) on the scale.

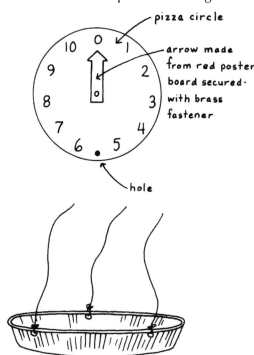

pizza circle

arrow made from red poster board secured with brass fastener

hole

Pie plate with three holes evenly spaced, three strings tied through holes

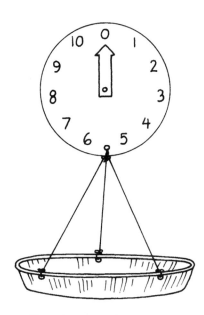

Tie strings in hole on pizza circle.

Barbecue Grill

3+

Social development

Social Studies

This prop fits into a camping, cowboys and cowgirls, food, summer or picnic theme.

Materials

✓ a box about 8" x 8" x 12" ✓ scissors
✓ cookie cooling rack ✓ twist ties
✓ twigs ✓ decorative self-adhesive paper
✓ tongs ✓ artificial meat props (optional)

What to do

Cutoff the box flaps.

Cover the box with self-adhesive paper.

Put the twigs inside the box.

Put the cookie rack on top of the box; use the twist ties to tie it in place.

A child can pretend to cook on the barbecue grill.

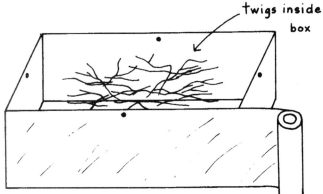

twigs inside box

Cover box with contact paper.
Punch hole in center of each side
close to top.

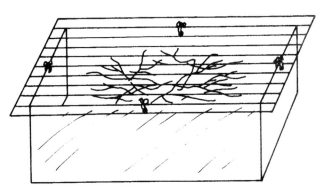

Secure cookie cooling rack to top of
box with twist ties.

Apple Tree

3+

Physical development

Social Studies

Use the Apple Tree during a farm, fall or harvesting theme. Apples can also be a separate theme.

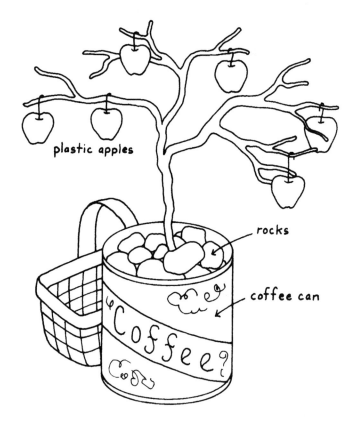

plastic apples

rocks

coffee can

Materials

✓ tree branch, 4' long   ✓ large coffee can
✓ small basket   ✓ rocks
✓ two dozen plastic apples (they are sold as Christmas tree ornaments and have hanging loops)

What to do

While holding the tree branch in the coffee can, fill it with rocks.

Hang the apples on the branches.

A child can pick the apples and put them in the basket or use the tree in another way while it is in the Dramatic Play Center.

Cotton Plant

3+

Language & Physical development

Social Studies

The Cotton Plant fits into a theme of plants, clothing or farms.

Materials

✓ branch from a tree with many small branches
✓ cotton balls
✓ scissors
✓ clear tape
✓ rocks
✓ precut green paper leaves
✓ egg cups (cut from an egg carton)
✓ large coffee can
✓ cloth bag

What to do

While holding the branch in the coffee can, fill it with rocks.

Make holes in the egg cups and put them on the ends of the twigs.

Tape the leaves on the branch.

Put the cotton balls inside the egg cups.

The children pick the cotton and put it in their bag.

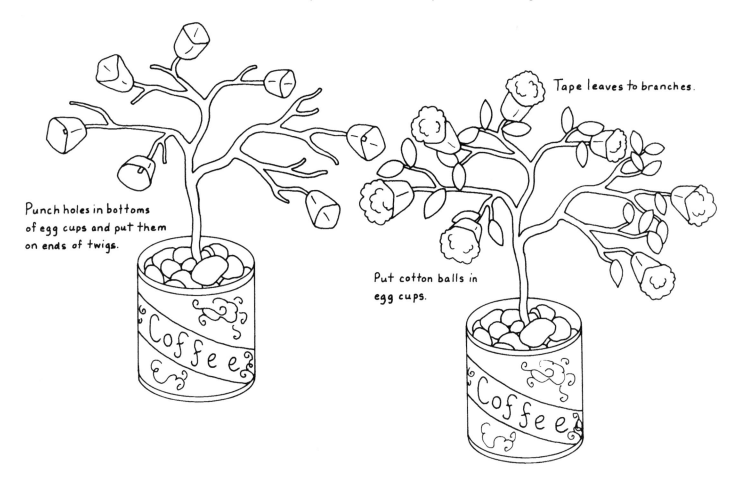

Punch holes in bottoms of egg cups and put them on ends of twigs.

Tape leaves to branches.

Put cotton balls in egg cups.

Lion Mask

3+

Physical development

Social Studies

The Lion Mask is a Dramatic Play Center prop that fits into a circus, pet or zoo theme.

Materials

✓ 20 to 25 strips of brown and yellow construction paper, 1" x 12"
✓ 1 brown grocery bag
✓ glue
✓ pencil
✓ marker
✓ scissors
✓ cardboard circle 6" in diameter

What to do

Trace around the cardboard circle with the marker 1" from top or bottom of the brown bag.

Cut out the circle.

Cut the shape shown in the illustration from the two sides of the bag.

Glue the shapes to the top two corners of the bag to make the ears.

Glue the yellow and brown strips around the hole in the bag.

Roll each strip around the pencil.

A child can wear the mask and pretend to be a lion.

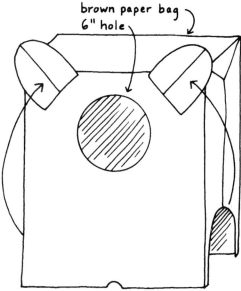

brown paper bag
6" hole

Cut shapes from sides
and glue to top to make ears.

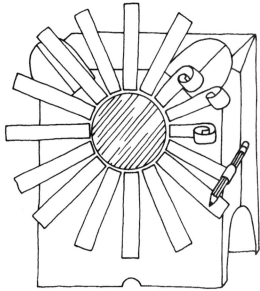

Glue yellow and brown strips around
hole in bag and roll each strip around
pencil to curl.

Bar Bell

3+

Physical development

Social Studies

The bar bell fits into a theme of the circus or unusual jobs.

Materials

✓ 1 gift-wrap cardboard tube
✓ newspaper
✓ marker
✓ 2 heavy duty rubber bands
✓ 2 white paper bags

white bakery paper bags
newspaper

50 lbs.   50 lbs.

gift wrap
cardboard cylinder

rubber bands

Stuff newspaper into each bag.

50 lbs.   50 lbs.

Pull rubber bands over the ends of
the bags to hold them on the cylinder.

What to do

Turn the bags so the open ends meet.

Write the weight on each bag.

Put the rubber bands on the cylinder.

Put the cylinders inside the two bags.

Stuff the bags with the newspaper.

Pull the rubber bands over the ends of the bags to hold them on the cylinder.

Put in the Dramatic Play Center and let the children's imagination take over.

Snowcone

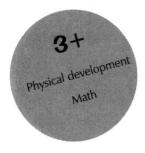

3+

Physical development

Math

The Snowcone fits into the themes of circus, summer or food. Children will learn more skills if they help in the construction of this play prop as well as any of the other props in this chapter.

Materials

✓ yarn
✓ cone-shaped paper cups
✓ cotton balls
✓ 3" x 3" piece of cardboard
✓ glue
✓ string

What to do

Begin by placing the string across the cardboard.

Wrap the yarn around the cardboard about 300 times.

Turn the cardboard over and cut the yarn down the middle.

Tie the string tightly.

Fill the cup half way with cotton balls.

Put glue on top of the cotton balls.

Dip the yarn ball in the glue and place it on the cotton balls.

Children can pretend to purchase a snowcone, sell a snowcone, eat a snowcone.

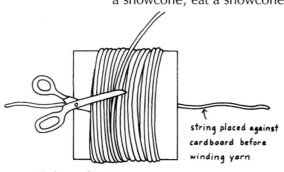

string placed against cardboard before winding yarn

Wind yarn 300 times around cardboard and cut down the middle.

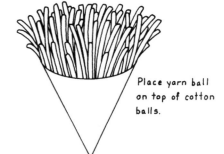

cone-shaped paper cup

Fill paper cup ½ full of cotton balls.
Apply glue to top of cotton balls.

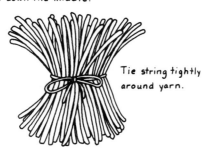

Tie string tightly around yarn.

Place yarn ball on top of cotton balls.

Space Helmet

3+

Language development

Social Studies

This prop fits into a space theme or it can be a part of a transportation unit that includes space travel.

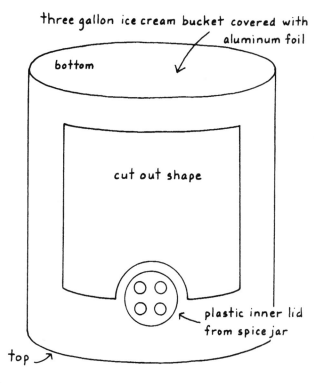

three gallon ice cream bucket covered with aluminum foil

bottom

cut out shape

plastic inner lid from spice jar

top

Materials

✓ 3-gallon ice cream bucket (usually found where ice cream is sold in bulk)
✓ aluminum foil
✓ plastic, inner lid with perforated holes (these are the "tops" through which spices and condiments are shaken, like crushed garlic or onion flakes)

What to do

Cut a hole in the ice cream container as shown in the illustration.

Glue aluminum foil to the container.

Glue the plastic lid in place.

Place in the Dramatic Play Center.

Air Pack

3+

Language & Physcial development

Social Studies

Space travelers will need Air Packs.

Materials

✓ 2 plastic tennis ball cans
✓ aluminum foil
✓ elastic
✓ hot glue gun

What to do

Using the hot glue gun, glue the two cans together.

Use the hot glue gun to burn holes in the bottom of the tennis ball cans by holding the gun point next to the plastic (but do not squeeze the trigger).

Thread the elastic through the holes and tie it off.

Place in the Dramatic Play Center.

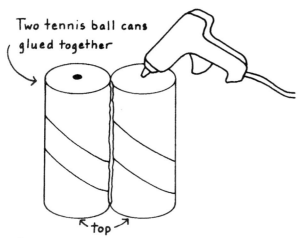

Two tennis ball cans glued together

top

Burn holes in can bottoms with glue gun. (do not squeeze trigger)

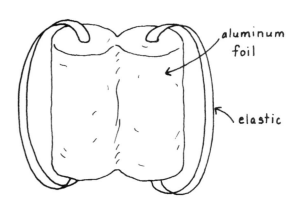

aluminum foil

elastic

Cover cans with aluminum foil. Thread elastic through holes and tie ends together.

Flippers

3+

Physcial development

Social Studies

Flippers fit into a beach or summer theme. However, with a little modification, they can become the webbed feet of different aquatic animals.

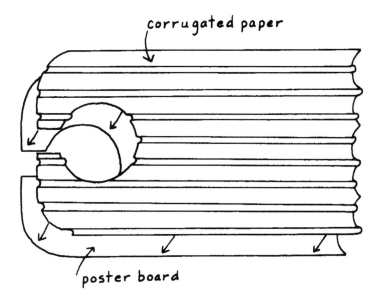

corrugated paper

poster board

Glue corrugated paper to poster board.

Materials

✓ corrugated, colored paper
✓ scissors
✓ glue
✓ piece of poster board

What to do

Cut out flipper shapes from the corrugated paper.

Glue the flippers to the poster board and cut them out again.

A child wears the flippers, like a swimmer.

Note: Make the flippers small so children will not trip while wearing them.

Life Vest

3+

Language & Physical development

Social Studies

The life vest is a Dramatic Play Center prop. It can be used with a transportation theme or a beach theme. It can also be used with a camping theme, focusing on recreational activities such as boating.

Materials

✓ sheet of poster board
✓ a shoe string
✓ scissors
✓ a hole punch
✓ thick yarn
✓ hole reinforcers
✓ marker

What to do

Cut out a back panel.

Cut out two front panels.

Punch holes in the back and front panels at the shoulders and at the sides.

Use hole reinforcers over each of the punched holes.

Tie the shoulders together with the thick yarn.

Tie the sides together with the thick yarn.

Punch holes in the front two panels.

Use hole reinforcers over the holes.

Use a shoe string to tie the panels together.

Draw a patch on the life jacket.

Children use the life jacket in their play.

Binoculars

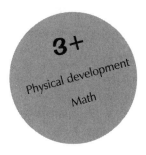

3+

Physical development

Math

Children love to make and use binoculars. They can be used with a camping, summer or senses theme.

Materials

✓ 2 toilet paper cylinders
✓ thick yarn
✓ glue

✓ aluminum foil
✓ scissors

What to do

Glue the two cylinders together.

Cover them both with aluminum foil.

Using the scissors, make holes in two sides of the cylinders.

Tie the thick yarn through the holes.

Place in the Dramatic Play Center.

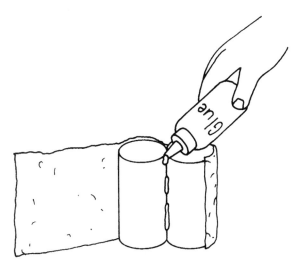

Glue together two toilet paper cylinders.
Cover them both with aluminum foil.

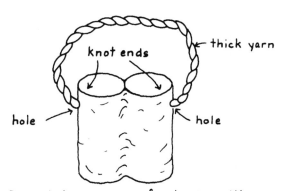

Punch holes in sides of cylinder with scissors and thread thick yarn through holes, secure with a knot.

Hula Skirt

3+

Physical development
Social Studies

While a Hula Skirt is a good prop for a beach theme, it is also a great prop for fun at any time.

Materials

✓ 2 sheets of newspaper
✓ wide masking tape
✓ green marker
✓ velcro

What to do

Color the newspaper green with the marker.

Tape the two sheets together, layering them.

Cut the layered newspaper into 1″ strips.

Affix the soft-side of a velcro strip on one side of the skirt and the hook-side on the other.

Place in the Dramatic Play Center.

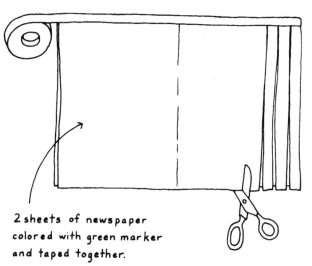

2 sheets of newspaper colored with green marker and taped together.

Cut one inch strips.

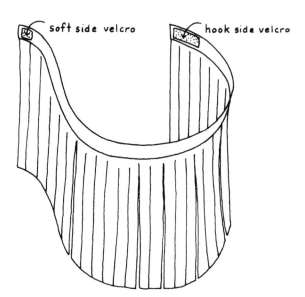

soft side velcro   hook side velcro

Affix soft side velcro on one side of the skirt waistband and hook side velcro on the other. (A longer velcro strip on one side will make skirt adjustable.)

Chapter 5

The Library Center

The Library Center is the heart of the classroom. Why? Because literacy skills are so critical. However pushing young children to learn to read before they are developmentally ready (making them miss the enjoyment of prereading), would be an unfortunate mistake. The activities in this chapter help make learning to read a pleasure.

Library Center tools are books, paper, pencils and markers. We want children to love books. We want them reading, writing, speaking and listening. The Library Center is the place for children to have fun, meaningful interactions with books and print so that they will develop these skills. Many different skills are developed in the Library Center, a major learning place for young children.

Listening

At the listening center, children can choose among tapes and books. It is very satisfying to watch children respond to simple prerecorded directions. They hear new speech sounds, word patterns and vocal tones that express different feelings. While listening to tapes they begin to recognize and compare familiar and unfamiliar sounds. Children have the opportunity to listen to other children read their own crated stories.

Reading

When children hear good stories that are either read or told, they begin to understand that books are an integral part of life. However, books are meaningful and inviting when they relate to the children's experiences. By exposing children to books, they learn that books have a beginning and an end, and that something happens in the middle. They begin moving their eyes from the left of the page to the right, and from the top of the written message to the bottom. These are two important skills that need to be acquired for children to learn to read. Children also "read" the pictures for clues to the text and make up their own stories using the pictures. Another important thing that children understand when exploring books is that symbols on the page—pictures and letters on the page—stand for something and that all of it has implications for speech and the framing of ideas. When they understand that each letter means something special they have reached the representational level in reading. Books give children the opportunity to retell a familiar story in their own way, to respond to various forms of literature, to follow simple story lines and to predict outcomes. Giving them opportunities to retell favorite stories, helps children to begin to think sequentially. This skill is also essential for reading. Children need to be able to sequence letters in order to read a word; sequence words to read a sentence; and, most of all, sequence thoughts to make stories. Reading is learning to extract meaning from print.

Writing

Reading and writing are two sides of the same coin. Young children learn both reading and writing in similar ways. They both are language processes. While reading and writing happens in all the centers, in the Library Center children create their own stories using invented spelling or conventional writing. They experiment with print using various writing tools. Children become aware of spaces between words and of those funny marks on the paper—punctuation—that are not letters, but that have a purpose in clarifying what words mean. They learn word patterns and configurations. They observe and learn that words come in different lengths. All of these occur because children have lots of opportunities to write and to examine print.

Speaking

Children sometimes need a reason to talk. A good book or their own written stories, give children an opportunity to speak purposefully and that makes them feel important. Children learn language by using it. By listening to stories, children hear language occurring; and, they will model, often silently for awhile, what they hear. After many opportunities a child will begin to feel comfortable with speaking what they hear and express it out loud. Another way to encourage talking is to set up a tape recorder into which the children read or tell stories. Collect old tapes that you no longer use. Place these in a basket next to the tape recorder and teach the children how to record their stories. They can record their voices over and over again. Children like listening to themselves. Include a puppet area in the Library Center. Children who might not otherwise express themselves will do so when given a chance to speak for someone else. To learn to speak, children must practice. It follows that they be given opportunities to do so.

Creating the Library Center

Since it is the heart of the classroom, the Library Center needs to be carefully planned and set up in such a way as to be an inviting and comfortable place for children. First, choose an area that is removed from the main traffic pattern, in a relatively quiet part of the room. Look around and make sure you have access to electrical outlets.

The furniture needs will depend on the space available. An essential piece is the book display. If you have lots of space, get an old bathtub or plastic wading pool and fill it with pillows. Line up the books against the wall and the tub so the children can see their choices. If you have a small space use resealable, plastic bags to display the books. Place one book in each bag. Hang the bags from a clothesline that is nailed flush against the wall. Use clothespins to hold the bags with the books. The children take down a bag, get out the book and read it. When they are finished they return it to the bag and clip it back on the clothesline. A small, inclined library book display shelf works well, too. The important thing is that the children can see the book selections.

The next consideration is a place to sit and to read. A beanbag chair, large pillows, a rocking chair or the bathtub mentioned above (pillows included) all work well. Children are invited to this area when they see a soft, comfortable setting.

On the library shelf, include a wide selection of books that relate to the children's interest and experiences. If you are talking about the fire fighters, for example, be sure to include books about the topic. Keep other books on the shelf, too, since the children will want to pursue other topics. If you have space, have one shelf called "Topic of the Week" and another shelf for favorites. Make sure you have "wordy" books for children who are ready for them, picture books for those who are not and some of average reading difficulty.

Be sure to include a variety of writing materials and activities in the Library Center. Because the children will be writing, they need a writing table and chairs if there is room. If not, make sure you have several clipboards and carpet squares on which the children can sit. This will define their work-space. The clipboard gives them a solid surface on which to write. To create the writing section of the Library Center, place a selection of writing activities on the bookshelf so the children will have choices depending on their writing ability. Place the materials needed for each activity in a basket, on a tray or in a dish tub. The child chooses a writing activity, takes it to the table, works it and returns it to the shelf. For suggestions on things to make available to encourage writing, see the activities in this chapter. There are many things on which the children can write, including unlined newsprint, lined and unlined paper, construction paper, transparencies, stationery, cardboard, magic slates, memo boards, carbon paper, junk mail, computer paper, notepads, graph paper, textured paper, order forms, receipts, calendars, chalkboard, dry erase boards, newspaper and notebooks. There are many things to write with, including crayons, pencils, pens, chalk, colored pencils, soap crayons, markers, alphabet stamps, magnetic letters, dry erase markers, roll-on bottles, feathers and bingo markers. And, there are a variety of things to write in, including a shallow box of sand, a cafeteria tray with shaving cream or fingerpaint, a shallow tray of sawdust, a cafeteria tray with toothpaste or colored liquid soap.

The listening center, another area of interest, works best on a small table with two or three chairs to limit the number of children able to use it at any one time. If you have any of the other equipment, each piece needs to have its own small table and work space. At the listening center, put the books and the related tapes in individual, clear, resealable, plastic bags and place the bags in a large basket. The children can see the books through the bag and they will not have to remove them to see their choices. Include four to six choices. Change them when you see the children have grown tired of the selections available. Make sure you have a range of selections that meets the individual ability levels and needs of the children.

Other materials to include in the Library Center are the flannel board, magnet board and a puppet space. What you include depends on the space available. If space is limited include them on a rotating basis.

The Library Center needs to be a stimulating, yet efficient place, organized so children can draw, write, listen to stories, create their own stories and books, read books and learn other ways to interact with written print.

Blank Story Books

3+

Reading
& Writing

Sometimes children need to be inspired to start writing stories. Having a selection of blank books may get them started.

Materials

- ✓ colored construction paper
- ✓ scissors
- ✓ newsprint
- ✓ stapler
- ✓ markers and pencils
- ✓ basket

What to do

To make blank books, start simply. For the cover, cut out basic shapes from colored construction paper. Rectangles, ovals, squares, circles and triangles make easy, simple book covers.

Cut newsprint to fit the cover shape for the inside pages.

Staple them together.

At first, put two or three sheets inside the book cover. A thick book is intimidating.

After the children have started writing books, cut out unusual shapes like ice cream cones, cars, trees, animal silhouettes. Make blank books to go along with themes. This sometimes is a reason for children who do not generally write stories to write one.

Place all the books in a basket with a container of pens and writing tools. Put the basket on the shelf, near the writing table.

Note: When the children are comfortable creating stories with small books, make blank big (oversized) books available. The children can write the book as a class project or individually.

Velcro Book

3+

Reading & Writing

For children who are not comfortable writing a story, this activity gives them a way to be invited into the process of creating a story in a fun way.

Materials

✓ large sheets of soft side velcro (car interior shops are a good source)
✓ scissors
✓ fabric glue
✓ hole punch
✓ notebook rings
✓ flannel board pieces
✓ tray
✓ small basket

What to do

Cut the sheets of velcro into four sheets, 22" x 10".

Fold in half along the 22" dimension, creating two 11" x 10" pages (velcro soft-side facing outward). Use fabric glue and seal the two backs together.

When you have the pages made, use a hole punch and punch holes in the nonfolded side (in other words, the holes will be opposite the folded edge of the velcro). Put the book together with notebook rings inserted through the holes.

Place the book on a tray along with a small basket of flannel board pieces including animals, trees, toys and people. If you do not have flannel board pieces, cut out small pictures from magazines, glue them on tagboard, cut them out and put a small piece of hook-sided velcro or a small piece of sandpaper on the back. The children use the books and the story pieces to create their own stories.

Baggie Book

3+

Reading
& Writing

This is an excellent way to make a book that can be used again and again.

Materials

✓ resealable, plastic sandwich bags   ✓ colored masking tape
✓ clear cellophane tape   ✓ basket
✓ pieces of tagboard and blank paper cut to fit inside the baggie

What to do

Tape the end opposite the bag opening to a work table with clear cellophane tape.

Place the next baggie on top of the first and tape it to the table. Repeat with the third and fourth baggie.

Pull up the layered book of baggies from the table and fold over the tape to the reverse side of the baggies.

Use the colored tape to make the binding. Affix the tape evenly along the front and back; seal the entire length of the baggie book. Slide the precut tagboard pages into each baggie. You will want to make several.

Place the baggie books and blank sheets of paper in a basket on the writing activity shelf.

The child writes a story and illustrates it on the precut pages, then slides the story into the baggie book.

When the children have lost interest in that story, the baggie book is ready to be used for the next story.

Note: For longer stories try making baggie books from 2-gallon, reasealable, plastic bags.

A special thanks to Dianne Hill for this idea.

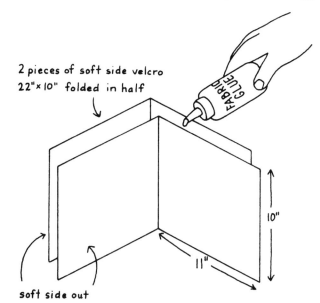

2 pieces of soft side velcro
22"x 10" folded in half

10"

11"

soft side out

Use fabric glue to seal the two sides together. Make two sets.

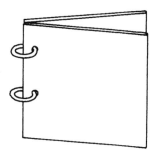

Punch holes in the unfolded edges of the pages and join together with notebook rings.

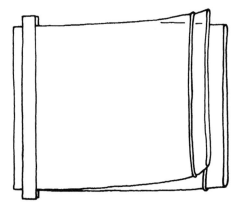

Tape baggie to work surface. Tape second baggie over first. Repeat with third and fourth baggie.

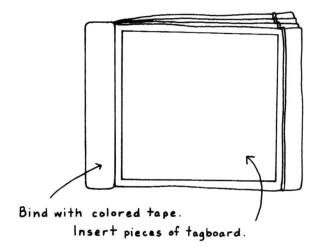

Bind with colored tape.
    Insert pieces of tagboard.

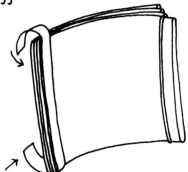

Pull up layered baggies and fold excess tape to reverse side.

Insert story pages.

Photo Album

3+

Reading

Speaking

Children love to look at pictures of themselves. In this activity it gives them a reason to read the picture descriptions, trying to understand what is being said about the picture. They learn that the words and the pictures, capture the same experience, one helping the other to improve the clarity of what is being described.

Materials

✓ pictures of the children
✓ album
✓ pens or markers

What to do

Start a class photograph album by taking pictures of the children in all the aspects of the classroom and of the special classroom activities.

As the pictures are added to the album during the school year, have the child in the photograph dictate a sentence about it.

The children will choose to read this book over and over. As time passes, the children can write words or sentences about themselves.

At the end of the year, take the book apart and send a photograph with the child's description home with each child.

Mail Station

3+

Reading & Writing

Having another opportunity for children to communicate with you and with another is important. How? Through the mail.

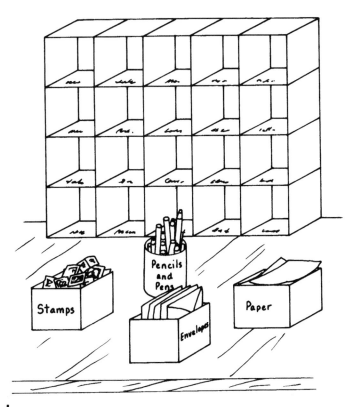

Materials

✓ 1/2 gallon milk or juice cartons   ✓ scissors
✓ brads   ✓ markers
✓ decorative self-adhesive paper or aluminum foil
✓ junk mail, envelopes, paper, crayons
✓ markers, blank paper and magazine stamps
✓ baskets

What to do

Set up a mail station in the Library Center.

Take 1/2 gallon milk or juice cartons and cut off the tops.

Use brass fasteners to attach each carton to the next, four or five cartons across and four or five cartons deep.

When all of the cartons are attached, cover them with decorative self-adhesive paper or aluminum foil.

Note: Be sure to cover all sharp edges.

Put a child's name on each box and, if you have school pictures, photocopy them and place each child's photograph above their name. Leave the photos for several weeks until the children recognize each other's names.

Encourage them to write letters to each other. When they know each other's names, remove the pictures.

Save old Valentine envelopes and junk mail envelopes. Place them in a basket.

In another basket place small sheets of paper for letter writing. In a third basket place magazine stamps. These are perfect for the children to lick and stick on the envelopes to mail their letters.

Place the three baskets on the writing shelf. Children will enjoy corresponding with their friends. Do not forget to have a mail box for yourself so the children can write letters to the teacher.

Reading Bags

3+

Listening
Reading
Speaking

Since children have different learning styles and interests, it is necessary to have lots of choices prepared. This increases the possibility of motivating a child who has not shown interest in writing or reading. This activity probably will reach most unmotivated children.

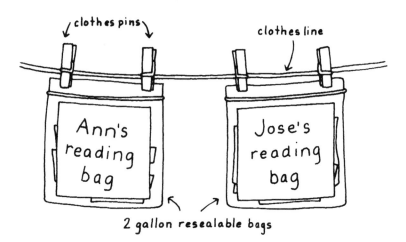

Materials

✓ clothespins
✓ clothesline
✓ resealable, 2-gallon plastic bags, one for each child

What to do

Use clothespins to attach resealable, 2-gallon plastic bags on a clothesline that has been attached to a wall. Have a bag for each child.

When a child eats something special, feeds a pet, buys her favorite cookies, goes to McDonald's to eat, buys a toy or gets new shoes, have her bring the label, logo, trademark, bag, wrapper or box to school.

Have her put it in her plastic reading bag.

The collection process will also get the parents involved.

You might need to limit the size of the items to one that will fit inside the bag.

The child reads her labels to anyone who will listen. When the bag gets too full, you might make the child a Reading Book either by gluing or stapling the labels on pages; or, for the older children scripting it with them. For example: I like _____. I feed the birds _____. I bought new shoes at _____.

Reusable Book

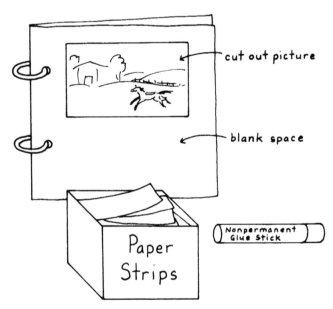

Some children are not ready to illustrate stories. They need ways to take the initial steps that accept the child "where he is," and get him involved in print, comfortably.

Materials

✓ old calendars, textbooks, magazines
✓ blank paper
✓ strips of paper
✓ basket

✓ scissors
✓ glue
✓ nonpermanent glue

What to do

Cut out pages from old calendars, textbooks or magazines.

Purchase glue sticks that are not permanent.

Create a picture book with these pictures, leaving about 5" of vertical space at the bottom of each page for some script that will be written on writing strips.

Create a pictorial picture sequence for the children. It will help them create a story with their written words.

Cut writing strips 4 1/2" high and as wide as the book page. These strips are going to be used for the story script when a child wants to write it.

Place the strips in a basket with a stick of nonpermanent glue.

As the child goes through the book, he writes a story line for each illustrated page on the writing strip.

He puts the glue on the back of the strip and sticks it on the story page.

When he has scripted the entire book, has read his story to his friends, he can then remove his script and take it home. The picture book is available for the next child to write his story.

Accordion Books

3+

Reading & Writing

This is another way to attract children who may not be enthusiastic about reading and writing.

Materials

✓ paper
✓ scissors
✓ pens, markers, pencils, crayons
✓ basket

What to do

Cut long, narrow strips of paper 20" x 6".

Fan-fold the paper strips in 5" folds making sure the folds open as does the book.

The child uses the front as the cover, and writes on the inside of the folds continuing on the back if they have a lot to say.

Place the premade books in a basket on the writing shelf, along with writing tools.

Give the child a sticker to seal their books when they get ready to take them home or if the book is a secret document.

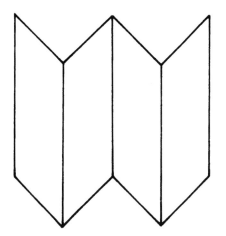
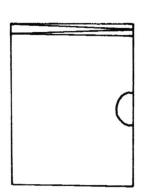

Sequence Cards

3+

Listening
Writing
Speaking

Since children need to know how to sequence to learn how to read, sequencing activities like this one are needed in all the centers, especially the Library Center.

Materials

✓ photocopier
✓ crayons
✓ tagboard
✓ basket

✓ story book
✓ glue
✓ clear self-adhesive paper

What to do

Take a favorite story of the children and photocopy a set of three pictures that emphasize the progression of the story.

Color the pictures, glue them to tagboard, laminate them or cover them with clear self-adhesive paper and place them in a basket on the writing shelf.

The children will enjoy retelling the story using the cards as prompts.

Once they are comfortable with a three-picture sequence, do another story in a four-picture sequence and another in a six-picture sequence.

Talk About Cards

3+

Listening
Reading
Speaking

This activity gives the children a reason to talk and it helps them recall story events.

Materials

✓ story books
✓ glue
✓ self-adhesive paper
✓ basket
✓ cookie sheet

✓ photocopier
✓ tagboard
✓ scissors
✓ magnetic tape
✓ tape recorder

What to do

Choose one of the children's favorite stories. Find two illustrations in the book: one that depicts the beginning and one that depicts the end. You can use any two things in the story that can be compared by the children: up and down, light and dark, inside and outside, same and different.

Photocopy the two illustrations, color them, glue them to a piece of tagboard, laminate or cover with clear self-adhesive paper and cut them out.

Put a strip of magnetic tape on the back of the illustration cards.

Use a cookie sheet as a magnet board. The children stick the cards on the magnet board.

Set up a small area for the children to work with this activity. Place the magnet board, the basket of cards and a tape recorder with blank tape in the workspace.

The children use the cards, talking about them into the tape recorder. When children enjoy other stories that lend themselves to talk about cards, make them and add them to the basket.

Story Puzzle

3+

Listening & Reading

Children love puzzles, especially those that relate to the things that interest them.

Materials

✓ children's books
✓ markers
✓ self-adhesive paper

✓ photocopier
✓ scissors
✓ resealable, plastic bag

What to do

Select a favorite book and photocopy one significant page of the story.

Make two copies; color both of them identically. One will be the puzzle base and the other will be cut into puzzle pieces.

Cut the puzzle into the number of pieces the children can manage. Trace each puzzle piece onto the base to create an outline of each puzzle piece so that the children can see the shape of each piece.

Laminate or cover the base with self-adhesive paper.

Place the pieces in a resealable, plastic bag on the writing shelf.

When the children work with the puzzle they will be reviewing the story.

Sand Writing

4+

Reading & Writing

Many younger children are sensory learners. They need to have touch and feel activities.

Materials

✓ small shallow box
✓ glue

✓ colored fluorescent paper
✓ sand

What to do

Create a sand box for writing.

Cover the inside bottom of a small shallow box with colored fluorescent paper. Glue it well, especially around the edges.

Cover the bottom of the box with a 1″ layer of sand.

The children use their fingers to write or move their fingers in the sand. The fluorescent paper reveals clearly the results of their work. Exploring this activity establishes a basic skill used for writing.

Textured Letters and Numerals

4+

Reading
& Writing

Children have different learning styles. Some children need to touch things to understand them. Sensory experiences, such as feeling letters and numerals, are enjoyed by all children but essential for sensory learners. This activity takes about two days to complete, so you will have to plan this one in advance. This activity is best for older children.

Materials

✓ 3" x 5" index cards
✓ markers
✓ glue
✓ bird grit
✓ basket

What to do

Trace each letter on a 3" x 5" index card.

Make the letters and numerals about 1/2" wide.

Spread glue on one letter or numeral at a time.

Sprinkle the glue with fine crushed bird grit (it can be purchased anywhere bird food is sold).

Set the letters aside to dry. It will take about two days.

Place the numerals and letters in a basket and place the basket on the writing shelf. When the children want to make a certain letter or numeral encourage them to find it among the other letters and numerals in the basket and to trace the outline several times with their fingers. This activity will help them to be able to write it.

Letter Stamping

4+

Reading & Writing

Children, especially older children, like to experiment using different tools to illustrate or embellish their stories, or to create different effects to tell their stories.

Materials

✓ carpet padding or flat sponges
✓ scissors
✓ thread spools or empty film canisters
✓ glue or hot glue gun
✓ stamp pad
✓ blank story pads
✓ basket

What to do

Letter stamps are easy and fun for children to use.

Cut out the letters of the alphabet from carpet padding or from flat sponges.

Glue the letters to empty thread spools or empty film canisters using a hot glue gun.

Place the letter stamps in a basket along with a stamp pad and blank story books for exploring letters.

Word Bracelet

4+

Reading & Writing

Children enjoy combining letters to make words. The following activity is a fun way for children to create a word and to wear it. Words can be conventional or invented. The goal is not to teach them to spell; rather, to experiment with words and to become familiar with letter and number patterns.

Materials

✓ empty cardboard, masking tape cylinders for the bracelets
✓ colored masking tape
✓ markers
✓ basket

What to do

Have enough bracelets for several of the vowels and of the more frequently used consonants.

Wrap each bracelet with colored masking tape.

On each bracelet, use markers to write a letter of the alphabet in several places around the bracelet.

Place the bracelets in a basket and place on the writing shelf.

The child selects bracelets to wear putting them on in sequence to spell an invented or a conventional word. Usually, they make their names and names of their friends.

Message Board

4+

Reading & Writing

Children learn that words are the principle way to communicate thoughts, ideas and feelings to others. Direct speech is one way. Written messages are another. A Message Board is one of the best ways to get them started.

Materials

✓ extra large cookie sheet
✓ pens, markers, pencils
✓ magnetic letters
✓ index cards
✓ basket

What to do

Purchase an extra large cookie sheet from a kitchen supply house. Attach it to a wall.

Place a basket of index cards and writing tools on the shelf close to the cookie sheet.

Also put a basket of magnetic letters on the shelf.

The children leave messages to their friends by writing on the index cards and sticking them on the cookie sheet with the magnetic letters.

They can also write their words with the magnetic letters.

Give the children reasons to write messages. Model leaving messages for different children at different times and for important occasions. An example might be: Marcos, do not forget to take your parent letter home. Also, leave messages announcing events that will occur that day. An example: Today is Ki's birthday.

If you need to bring something to school for some special activity, have a child write you a message on the message board. An example: Mrs. MacDonald, remember to bring the cream to make the ice cream.

Quill Writing

5+

Reading
& Writing

This is a fun activity that is best for older children.

Materials

✓ turkey feathers
✓ sharp knife (for teachers only)
✓ black paint
✓ tray
✓ sheets of paper

What to do

Collect several turkey feathers.

Take a knife and cut the blunt, nonfeathered end at an angle to make the pen point. Try not to make the point too sharp.

Place a small container of black paint on a tray with the quill and sheets of paper.

The child dips the quill in the paint and writes with it on paper. It is great fun. Children are drawn to this activity; it is another way that may inspire them to write.

Note: Try other types of feathers.

Publishing Box

5+

Listening
Reading
Speaking
Writing

This activity is for older children since it demands more developed fine motor skills. It introduces the children to the meaning of the words, publisher, author, illustrator, copyright and dedication.

Materials

✓ construction paper pieces in a file folder
✓ plain paper in a file folder
✓ stapler
✓ hole punch
✓ brads
✓ yarn pieces in a resealable, plastic bag
✓ large box or tote tray
✓ *How a Book Is Made* by Aliki (optional)

What to do

Place all the materials in a large box or tray and place on the shelf.

When the children decide to publish a book, it can be an individual or a group project.

After the book is written and illustrated with a title page, copyright date and a dedication page, it is ready for publishing. The children design a cover, write a brief summary to go on the back cover, write a page about the author for the inside of the back cover; and then they staple the book together.

They might want to use a hole punch and put the book together with brads or tie it together with yarn. A good book to use to get children started is *How A Book Is Made* by Aliki.

Note: If you want a picture of the author to display with the biographical information, make multiple copies of the children's school pictures on the copier. The children can cut out a picture of the author and glue it in the back of the book.

Overlay Book

5+

Reading
& Writing

This homemade book is for older children. It develops figure ground perception. The children have to be able to pick out many things in a busy background.

Materials

✓ white paper
✓ wallpaper pieces or construction paper
✓ clear laminating film or clear plastic report covers
✓ scissors
✓ stapler
✓ markers
✓ basket

What to do

To make the overlay book collect white paper for the pages, wallpaper pieces (or construction paper) for the cover, and clear laminating film or clear plastic report covers.

Cut four pages of paper for the book and cut the cover to fit.

Cut four pages of film to place on top of each page of the book.

Staple the whole book together. You will have one clear page and then a paper page, clear page, paper page throughout the book. Make many books as this is a very popular activity.

Place the premade books in a basket along with markers (usually permanent markers) that will write on the film page.

When a child chooses the basket he can draw a whole picture on two pages. Part will be on the film and the other will be on the paper. For example, he might draw the outside of an apple on the film and the inside of the apple on the paper. This is a challenge for the children.

Hint: It is much easier if the child starts drawing on the paper page and then works on the overlay page.

Note: This is a fun but difficult project for a class big book.

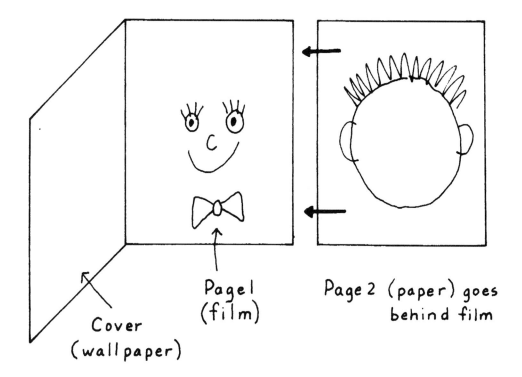

Cover
(wallpaper)

Page 1
(film)

Page 2 (paper) goes
behind film

Chapter 6

The Manipulative Center

Most classrooms already have a Manipulative Center; it may be called Table Toy Area, Games and Puzzles Center, Math Center. Whatever the name, the area offers children a quiet, calm place and time to do activities that either can be done alone, with a friend or with a small group of friends. Here are just a few of the things children can do in the Manipulative Center: work puzzles, string beads, make patterns, match, sort, classify items, stack, sequence, order things, work with shapes, colors and count objects. This is the Center where children work with all kinds of activities, pulling knowledge together from all curriculum areas, putting them to use in s tructured ways. Many of the activities, such as puzzles, sequence cards, stacking and nesting have self-correcting answers. Other activities offer opportunities for exploration and discovery like bead stringing. Activity selections should offer variety, as well as a range of difficulty. This enables all children, regardless of their ability, to be successful. Let's look at what can be learned.

Language Development: Reading, Writing, Speaking and Listening

When children work with pegboards, puzzles and matching and sorting objects, they are developing emergent reading skills, such as directionality and figure ground discrimination. When they use letter magnets to write their name, they are learning letter recognition. When they read food or toy labels brought from home and made into a game, they are developing their reading and writing skills. Often children choose to work with a friend on an activity. This gives them an opportunity to share their thoughts and ideas. The act of working together on a project provides structure and practice in taking turns, speaking and listening. New vocabulary is developed when children talk about what they are doing, how they are doing it and what happened when it was done.

Math and Science

So much of science is math and so much of math is science. If one is happening in the Manipulative Center, so is the other. When children sort, match, classify and sequence, they are observing and comparing. Both of these processes develop essential math and science skills. Children also develop an understanding of the properties of things when they manipulate objects in the Center. The idea that one thing has properties (characteristics) that make it different from all other things is a scientific concept. So, in many instances, as math happens so does science. Pattern or sequence cards give the children opportunities to work with sequences and patterns, essential math concepts. Patterning skills evolve when children use pegboards, string beads and when they use geoboards. Another valuable math skill is classification. The Manipulative Center is where children learn to classify things by descriptive attributes (colors, shapes, size), by generic characteristics (plants or animals) and by relationship (knife goes with spoon, chair goes with table).

Social Development

As a child works cooperatively with a friend or in a small group playing bingo, lotto or a matching game, she is developing social skills appropriate to group behavior. The skills of sharing and taking turns evolve when children work together in this Center. Patience, perseverance and tenacity are exhibited when a child completes a difficult puzzle. Self-confidence is developed as children feel they have been successful working with the different materials. They are more willing to try more challenging activities if they feel successful.

Physical Development

Fine motor skills are developed in the Manipulative Center. When children use the pegboard or geoboard, they are developing hand-eye coordination. When they use tweezers to move a piece of popcorn, for example, they are developing pincher control. As they crawl around on the floor working activities and they balance the puzzle to get it to their place, they are exercising their large muscles. When they move through the maze of other children working in the Center, they are learning about their body moving through space.

Creating the Manipulative Center

If the children are to choose this Center frequently, it needs to be an exciting place to work. It also needs to be arranged to facilitate their interaction with the objects and activities in an inviting way. How can a teacher do this? This is a fairly easy Center to locate in the classroom since it does not require water, electricity or a special floor covering. There is one consideration: the fewer distractions the better, so keep it in a quiet area of the classroom.

The primary furniture requirement is low, open shelving. The shelving will hold the activities and games to the children. You can use a table and chairs, but carpet squares also work. Have two carpet squares for each child able to use the Center. One is for sitting; the other defines workspace. The carpet square says: this is the working area; only certain pieces are placed here. Other activity pieces belong some where else. To use carpet squares, more classroom space is needed for the children to work since they spread-out on the floor.

When choosing materials to equip the Center, think about the ability levels of the children: what abilities do they possess and what abilities do you want them to develop. Some children need a very simple four-piece puzzle, while others need a fifteen-piece. Organizing from the easy to the complex is a constant challenge, but a rewarding one in that more children are usefully occupied and learning new skills. One way is to have activities that teach different skills rather than many activities teaching the same skill over and over. The following list of different activities will give the children a broad selection from which to choose.

✓ Seriation activities   ✓ Sequence activities

✓ Matching activities   ✓ Classifying activities

✓ Lacing shapes   ✓ Pegboard

✓ Geoboard   ✓ 1" colored cubes

✓ Bead stringing   ✓ Grouping activities

✓ Puzzles   ✓ Teacher-made folder games

✓ Nesting activities   ✓ Stacking activities

✓ Lotto, bingo, concentration and card games

✓ Self-help skill frames (buttoning, zipping, snapping and tying)

Place the activities on a tray, in a bucket, in a tote tray, a dish pan, a box or a tub. Then it is easier for the children to carry the activities to and from the shelves. It also gives them an organizing tool: all of these materials belong here, ready to be used and for storage after you are finished. When a child chooses the Center, he chooses an activity from the shelf, takes two carpet squares, sits on one, works on the other. When he is finished, he returns the activity to the shelf and starts all over again.

Rotate the activities as interest wanes. Put them away from time to time. Bring them out later. The children will be glad to see them. Change the materials as the children master the skills they teach, since they are no longer a challenge for the children. Put many easy puzzles out at the first of the year, but by late fall put most of them away and make available challenging puzzles to take their place (provided the children's skills have progressed). Throughout the year gradually increase the difficulty level of the puzzles as the children are ready for them. Avoid going back to retrieve a previously removed puzzle unless there is a specific child who needs it. Many times you will want to incorporate puzzles and other activities that relate to the current theme. This way, the materials changes as the theme changes.

The Manipulative Center is of great value in an early childhood classroom. Children enjoy the change of pace if affords, the variety and the different skill level challenges. It is the easiest center to maintain, especially if it is well planned and carefully organized for play.

Place Mat Puzzle

3+

Language & Physical development
Math & Science

This is an easy way to have a wide variety of puzzles at low cost. The difficulty level of the puzzles depends upon the ability level of the children. Children need to be challenged, but not intimidated; they need to feel successful.

Materials

✓ 2 identical placemats
✓ scissors
✓ markers
✓ resealable, plastic bag
✓ tray

What to do

Purchase two identical, plastic coated or sponge backed placemats. Use one for the base (which is the completed puzzle picture).

Cut the second puzzle into as many pieces as you feel the children can successfully manage to solve.

Take each piece and trace its outline on the base, so that you have an outline of each puzzle piece on the base. This makes it much easier for the children to work the puzzle.

Put the pieces in a resealable, plastic bag.

Place the base and bag with the pieces on a tray.

Put the tray on the shelf in the Center.

When a child chooses the activity, she takes the tray from the shelf, works the puzzle on the base and then she returns the material.

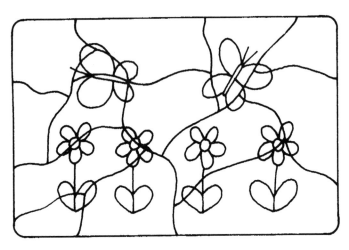

Geoboard

3+

Language & Physical
development
Math & Science

By making your own Geoboard, you can change the difficulty level of the board when the children are ready. Geoboard use is a wonderful way for children to develop figure/ground perception.

Materials

✓ sheet of pegboard
✓ box of small bolts and nuts
✓ fine blade saw (for teachers only)
✓ colored rubber bands
✓ small margarine tub
✓ tray

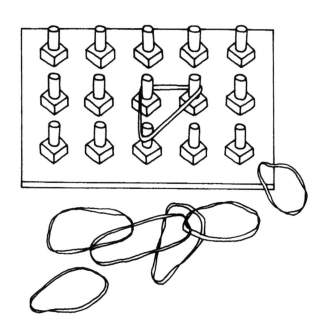

What to do

Purchase a sheet of pegboard and a box of small bolts and nuts (make sure the bolts fit the holes in the pegboard). These items can be purchased at most hardware stores.

Cut the pegboard into 12" x 12" squares.

Purchase colored rubber bands of different sizes and store them in a recycled small margarine tub.

To make the geoboard, push the bolts through all of the holes in the pegboard. Secure them with the nuts.

The top of the geoboard is the side with protruding bolt ends and nuts showing.

Place the geoboard and the tub of rubber bands on a tray. Place the tray on a shelf.

When a child chooses the activity, she uses the rubber bands to create designs, overlapping them on the bolts.

When she is finished, she takes off the rubber bands and replaces the materials on the shelf.

Note: If you would like the children to make specific designs, make geoboard pattern cards. They can make triangles, squares, hexagons and other shapes. Make a copy of the geoboard top on a copier. Use a marker to draw the design you want the children to make on the geoboard.

Shape Pictures

3+

Language development

Math & Science

Working with this activity, children use their creativity, imagining different organizations and developing figure/ground discrimination. This is also an excellent activity to recycle leftover construction paper.

Materials

✓ leftover construction paper
✓ scissors
✓ cardboard
✓ small box
✓ tray

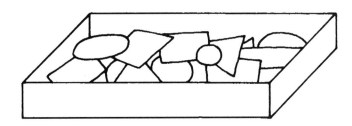

What to do

Cut all the leftover paper into geometric shapes like squares, circles, ovals, triangles, hexagons, pentagons and rectangles.

Cut a piece of cardboard about 12" square as a base on which to work.

Put all the paper pieces in a small box.

Put the box and the base on a tray.

Put the tray of the shelf.

When a child chooses the activity, she works on the base and uses the pieces to create a picture or design.

Playing Cards

3+

Language & Social
development
Math & Science

This is a versatile activity. The skills developed depend upon the age and ability level of the children.

Materials

✓ deck of cards
✓ basket

What to do

Purchase a deck of cards.

Place the cards in a basket and put the basket on the shelf in the Center.

When a child chooses the basket, he might do several things:

Match the cards by numbers

Put the cards in numerical order

Sort the cards by suits

Play Go Fish*

Play Battle*

Play Slap Jack*

Children who are ready will start adding or subtracting the numbers on the cards.

*Many children come to school knowing these games. To play Go Fish children must be able to recognize the numbers and names of the cards; Battle to know if a number is higher or lower; Slap Jack to recognize the same card and slap it before the other players do. The child that slaps the card first gets to take the whole stack of cards.

Clothespin Box

3+

Physical development

Math & Science

This is a very simple activity that encourages fine motor development and color matching skills. The narrower the strip of tape, the more challenging the activity becomes.

Materials

✓ clear plastic shoe box
✓ colored tape
✓ clothespins
✓ small basket

What to do

On a clear plastic shoe box, place several strips of colored tape at 2" intervals around the edge of the box.

Purchase clothespins that are the same color as the tape.

Place the pins in a small basket and place the basket inside the shoe box. Place the shoe box on the shelf.

When a child chooses the activity, she attaches the matching color clothespin on the tape. When she is finished she returns all the materials to the shelf.

Shoes

3+

Physical development

This activity provides opportunities for children to develop and improve their fine motor skills, using objects and materials that are meaningful, useful and important in their everyday lives.

Materials

✓ variety of shoes

What to do

Collect shoes that tie with laces, shoes that close with a velcro strap and shoes that close with a buckle.

Have the children practice closing each shoe. The velcro shoe is for those children who are not ready or able to tie or to buckle.

Card and Envelope Match

  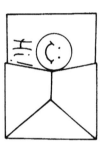

This is an activity that requires matching, visual discrimination and fine motor skills. The children also work with the size of materials.

Materials

✓ new or used greeting cards and envelopes
✓ baskets
✓ tray

What to do

Collect greeting cards. You will need various sizes and shapes, and the envelopes, as well.

Place the cards in a basket and the envelopes in another basket.

Place both on a tray in the Center. The children match the card to its envelope.

Ping-Pong Patterns

3+

Language development

Math & Science

This activity encourages children to create, repeat and extend patterns.

Materials

✓ 12 ping-pong balls
✓ 1 egg carton
✓ red and blue high-gloss enamel paint
✓ paper
✓ markers
✓ basket
✓ tray

What to do

Paint one side of six of the ping-pong balls red, creating red and white balls.

Paint one side of the other six ping-pong balls blue, creating blue and white balls.

Make pattern cards like the strips below using red, white and blue in the color schemes.

Place the pattern cards in a small basket, the balls in another small basket and the egg carton on a tray. Put the tray on the shelf.

When a child chooses the activity, he chooses a pattern card and creates his own pattern or duplicates a pattern card with the balls in the egg carton.

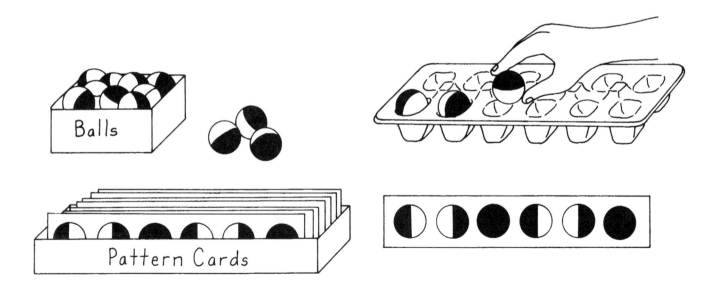

Lacing Shape

3+

Language & Physical development

Math & Science

This is another excellent activity for developing fine motor skills. Because the activity is made entirely by the teacher, it can be more or less difficult, depending on the skills of the children.

Materials

✓ different colors of poster board
✓ scissors
✓ hole punch
✓ boot shoe strings
✓ tray

What to do

Collect different colors of poster board.

Cut various shapes from the sheets like a circle, a star, a triangle and an oval. As a variation, cut out shapes that go with a theme like shoes, hats, bread or a car (for a transportation study, for example).

Use a hole punch and make holes, about 1″ apart, around the edge of the shape.

Purchase several long, boot shoe strings (72″ long at a minimum).

Place the shapes and the shoe strings on a large tray and place the tray on a shelf.

When a child chooses the activity, he laces the shape around the edge with the shoe string. When he finishes, he returns the materials to the shelf.

Note: If the children are very young make the shapes large and space the holes 3″ apart. With the older children, make the shapes smaller and the holes closer together.

Dog Biscuit Seriation

3+
Language development
Math & Science

This activity encourages the recognition of similarities and differences. Putting objects in order by size requires children to make comparisons.

Materials

✓ 3 sizes of dog biscuits
✓ black paper
✓ pen
✓ scissors
✓ tray
✓ tape
✓ margarine tub

What to do

Collect three sizes of dog biscuits.

Trace each size on black paper, creating a dog biscuit silhouette of each biscuit.

Divide a tray into four parts with tape.

Put a silhouette on three of the parts.

Put several of each size of the biscuits in a margarine tub and place the tub on the fourth space on the tray. Place the tray on the shelf.

When a child chooses the activity, she finds all the biscuits of the same size and puts them in the same place, matching biscuit size.

When the children learn about different sizes, change the activity by removing the silhouettes.

When they can do the activity without the silhouettes easily, remove the tape so the children can put the biscuits in order from largest to smallest, and from smallest to largest.

Note: This can be done with twigs, pencils, feathers, crayons, leaves, paper strips.

Cookie Cutter Matching

4+

Language development

Math & Science

This is a simple matching activity for younger children. It develops children's ability to see similarities and differences at a beginning level.

Materials

✓ cookie cutters
✓ pen
✓ large tray
✓ basket

✓ black paper
✓ scissors
✓ glue

What to do

Collect cookie cutters of various sizes and shapes. The more similar the cutters are, the more difficult the activity.

Trace each cookie cutter on black paper and cut them out.

Attach each silhouette to a large tray.

Put the matching cookie cutters in a basket on the tray. Place the tray on the shelf.

When a child chooses the activity, she matches the cookie cutter with its silhouette.

When she has matched all the cutters with their corresponding silhouettes, she returns the materials to the shelf.

Vehicle Sorting

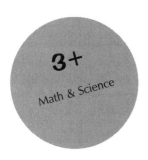

3+

Math & Science

This activity offers children opportunities to play with the most popular toys ever made (cars and trucks), but it also teaches about similarities and differences.

Materials

✓ cars and trucks
✓ large tray
✓ colored tape
✓ basket

What to do

Collect a variety of cars and truck that are similar in shape, like vans, semitrucks, pickup trucks, convertibles, sedans and race cars. The wider the selection, the more difficult the activity.

Divide a large tray into sections by applying colored tape. There needs to be a marked off section for each type of vehicle collected.

Place the vehicles in a basket and then on the tray. Put the tray on a shelf.

When a child chooses the activity, she finds all the vehicles that are alike and puts them in one section until all the vehicles have been sorted.

Note: These same vehicles can be sorted by color, number of wheels, number of doors.

Nesting

Nesting encourages the development of visual-perception skills. It can be made more or less difficult, depending on the skill level of the children.

Materials

✓ box lids (or jar lids, cans, plastic cups)
✓ tray

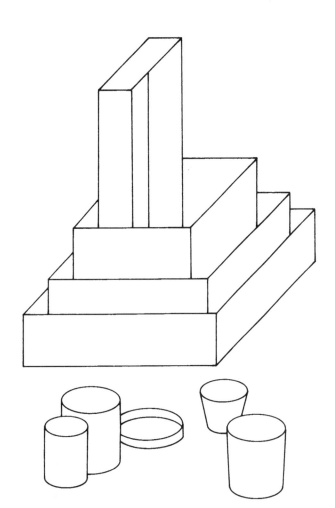

What to do

Collect box lids that fit one inside the other. Select as many lids as the children are able to work successfully, while still feeling challenged by the activity. Jar lids, cans and plastic cups work well for stacking, also.

Place the lids on a tray.

A child chooses the activity and puts the lids one inside the other until all of them fit.

Note: By using the materials differently, you can make this activity into a stacking activity.

Environmental Counting

4+

Language development
Math & Science

With this activity, children take an active role in creating what they do. Because of this, they are very motivated to work the activity. Environmental Counting improves children's number recognition and reading skills.

Materials

✓ boxes of products that have numerals on them
✓ large basket

What to do

Have the children bring boxes from home of products with numerals in the name, like 7-UP, V.O. 5, 9 Lives and V-8.

Get the children (and parents) involved collecting all of the home products with numerals from 1 to 10.

Place them in a large basket in the Center.

Have the children put them in numerical order. They can count backwards from 10, count by 2s or put objects in the box according to the numeral on it.

Leaf Sorting

4+

Language development
Math & Science

There are as many ways to do this activity as there are children in your classroom. Change it when the children tire of doing it one particular way.

Materials

✓ leaves
✓ basket
✓ colored tape
✓ self-adhesive paper or laminating film
✓ tray

What to do

Collect leaves of different shape, color and size.

Laminate each one or press them in clear self-adhesive paper.

Place the leaves in a basket on a tray divided into sections with colored tape. The children sort the leaves by size, color or shape.

For younger children put a silhouette on the tray to help the sorting process. For older children, make sure the leaves are similar but with enough variation to be sorted successfully.

Note: The children can sort twigs, crayons, bones, seeds, shoe strings, artificial flowers and puzzle pieces (from classroom puzzles with lost pieces).

Marble Design

This is an open-ended activity that offers children many opportunities to use their fine motor skills and to work on their patterning skills.

Materials

✓ old clean bath mat with suction cups on the back
✓ scissors
✓ clear plastic container
✓ marbles
✓ tray

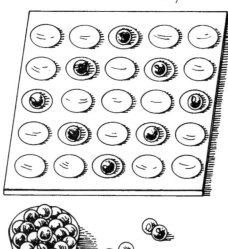

What to do

Cut the mat into a square.

Put the marbles in the container.

Place the marbles and the mat on a tray.

A child chooses the activity and places the marbles on the suction cups of the bath mat.

She can create a pattern, match the marbles or group them. If you have two of these activities, one child can copy another child's design.

Caution: Supervise closely any children who still put objects in their mouth.

Flower Parts

4+

Language development
Math & Science

Children explore part/whole relationships with this activity.

Materials

✓ boot box   ✓ felt
✓ hot glue gun   ✓ scissors
✓ 12" x 12" piece of soft-sided and hook-sided velcro

What to do

Cut the soft-sided velcro sheet to fit inside the boot box lid and glue it in place using a hot glue gun.

Cut large flower-part pieces from the felt: several flower heads, leaves, stems and roots.

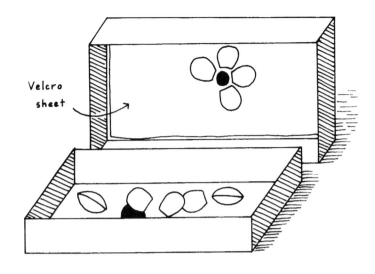

Velcro sheet

Put small pieces of hook-sided velcro on the back of each flower part.

Store the pieces inside the box.

Children select the box from the shelf and assemble the flower parts on the soft-sided velcro sheet on the inside of the box lid. Use this same velcro assembly format with any flannel board activity you create.

Magnet Board Game

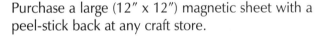

4+
Language development
Math & Science

The children can learn matching, classifying, patterning or seriation with this activity, depending on the materials you use.

Materials

✓ large magnetic sheet with a peel-stick back
✓ boot box or other large box
✓ metal cookie cutters

What to do

Purchase a large (12″ x 12″) magnetic sheet with a peel-stick back at any craft store.

Collect a boot box and metal cookie-cutters.

Peel off the back of the magnetic sheet and press it onto the shoe box lid.

Put the cutters in the box.

The children use the lid as the magnet board.

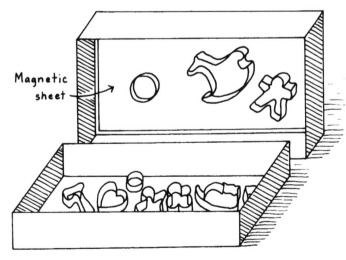

Magnetic sheet

The cookie cutters selected will determine the type of activity created. For example, to develop matching skills, select cutters that match. To develop classifying skills, select cutters that are topic related, like farm animal cutters, circus animal cutters, pets, tools or toy cutters. To develop patterning skills, select several cutters of each kind, so that the children can make patterns and repeat them. To develop seriation skills, select cutters that are different sizes.

Feel and Find Box

4+

Language & Physical development

This is a different approach to the "feely" box. It takes that activity one step further.

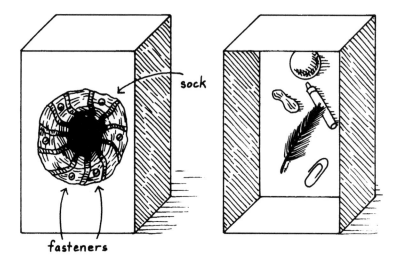

sock

fasteners

Materials

- ✓ 2 shoe boxes
- ✓ old sock
- ✓ scissors
- ✓ tray
- ✓ self-adhesive paper
- ✓ variety of small objects (2 of each object)
- ✓ brass fasteners

What to do

Cut a 3 1/2" hole in the lid of one of the shoe boxes.

Cover the box with self-adhesive paper and cut out the hole again.

Cut off the sock about 7" from the top, creating a tube.

Put the tube inside the hole in the box and fan-out the outer edge of the sock around the hole.

Use brass fasteners to hold the sock edge in place around the hole (see illustration).

Place one set of objects inside this box.

Place the matching set inside the other box and throw away the lid.

Place the closed box (with the attached sock) and the open box on a tray in the Center.

A child reaches inside the sock and feels the items. He selects a particular item, but before he pulls it out, he looks in the open box to find the matching item. When he has it in his hand, he pulls out the item and compares both. If they match, he sets them aside on the tray. If they don't match he puts them back in the boxes and tries again.

All Purpose Graph

4+

Language development

Math & Science

The following activity is an easy way for children to graph what they want to graph, when they want to graph it. They can do it the way they want to do it.

Materials

✓ foldout cutting board
✓ black permanent marker

What to do

Purchase a foldout, material cutting board from a fabric store. It will measure 72" x 40". One side has 1" squares across the entire board. The other side is blank.

Use a black permanent marker to make 8" x 8" squares that fill the blank side of the board. You will have nine squares across and five down. This gives the children two sides to use for graphing.

They can graph small items on the side with the small squares—coins, pebbles, animal crackers, M&Ms®, buttons, cubes, colored chips.

Caution: With young children who still put things into their mouths, be sure items are large enough so that they cannot be swallowed.

They can graph larger items on the other side—rocks, keys, bottles and jars, boxes, leaves, red, green and yellow apples, pictures, stuffed animals, flowers.

The children use the graph board by placing it flat on the floor.

Note: Boards come in different sizes. You can use any size. The larger the board, the easier it is for the children to use it effectively. Discourage the children from standing on it. It crushes easily.

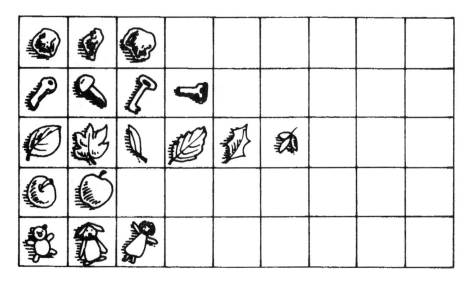

Peanut Grouping

4+

Math & Science

Peanut Grouping requires sorting by more than one characteristic. It is an important cognitive skill for children to develop. Because of its difficulty, it is best suited for older children.

Materials

✓ peanuts in the shell
✓ 3 embroidery hoops

What to do

Collect a variety of peanuts in shells and three embroidery hoops.

The children group the peanuts in the hoops according to the observed characteristics on the peanut shells.

Note: To make this activity easier, group objects that are more distinctive, like shells, feathers or rocks, and use only two hoops.

Pompom Toss

4+

Physical development

Math & Science

This is an excellent way to teach numeral recognition. If the children are ready, they will start combining numbers.

Materials

✓ old ice tray
✓ pompoms
✓ tray

✓ markers
✓ small margarine tub

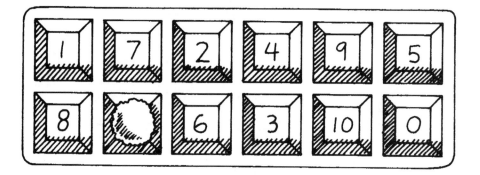

What to do

Find an old ice tray and write numerals 0 through 10 randomly in bottom of each compartment.

Purchase several large pompom balls (about 1/2" in diameter) and store them in a small margarine tub.

Place the ice tray and the margarine tub on a tray.

Place the tray on the shelf.

When a child selects the activity, she tosses the pompoms into the tray and checks the number of the compartment holding the pompom.

When finished, she returns the activity to the shelf. If two children play, they usually develop a method to keep score.

Box Puzzle

5+

Language & Physical development

This is a difficult puzzle, best for older children. Because it is made of recycled materials it is far less costly, yet really challenging. Children learn that reused materials can be put to very good use.

Materials

✓ 2 identical boxes with matching tops
✓ scissors

Collect two identical boxes with matching tops.

Put one box aside. It will be used as the puzzle base and the puzzle piece container.

The second box will be used to make a puzzle. Remove all of the sides of the second box. You should be left with a matching top to the first box.

Cut the top into as many pieces as you feel the children can solve, yet be successful.

Store the pieces in the first box.

Place the box containing the puzzle pieces on a tray on the shelf.

When a child chooses the activity, he works the puzzle on top of the base box.

When he is finished, he returns the pieces to the box and returns it to the shelf.

Photo Puzzle

5+

Language & Physical development

The photo puzzle is the most difficult for the children because there is no base on which the children can work. Surprisingly, however, this has been a high interest activity custom made for the class.

Materials

✓ enlarged photographs of the children at play
✓ tagboard or cardboard
✓ glue
✓ scissors
✓ large resealable, plastic bag
✓ blank paper and markers (optional)

Take a variety of photographs of the children at play. Enlarge them when they are developed.

Glue the photos to tagboard (or cardboard) to make them more sturdy.

Cut the photos into as many pieces as you feel the children can manage.

Store the photo pieces in a large resealable, plastic bag.

Place the bag on a tray.

If the puzzle solution proves to be too difficult for the children, trace the pieces on blank paper (creating a puzzle base). The children can use the traced shapes for reference in solving the puzzle.

Put the tray on the shelf.

Note: Do the same thing with old bulletin board decorations, magazine pictures and hardback book covers.

The Motor Center

Kids love to move! When children walk, tumble, roll, run, jump, stretch and bend they are developing major muscle groups and they are discovering their capabilities and limits of their bodies. Movement allows children to express their moods and emotions: swinging their arms, throwing a ball, stomping their feet or by running a race.

They can incorporate drama in their motor play, expressing their creativity, making characterizations and pretend movements. Teachers who understand this, incorporate movement activities in the curriculum, since it is such an important aspect of young children's development.

Children develop from their head to their toes using the large muscles first, and then they gradually master the refined abilities through the use of fine motor or small muscle skills. Learning motor skills helps children develop a sense of control, and it helps foster a positive self-image. Having a Motor Center in the classroom is an extremely valuable addition for young children.

Body Awareness and Image

As children work in the Motor Center, they learn what their bodies are capable of doing. They learn about the limits of their strength, their endurance and their body flexibility. Managing their bodies in a variety of settings builds self-confidence and a positive body image. A positive body image is important because we want to teach children to take care of themselves through proper personal hygiene and nutrition. If children like their bodies they are more likely to take care of them through proper diet and good personal health habits. In the Motor Center children learn how their bodies work and they learn the function of all the parts. They learn, for example, that one side of their body is different from the other, but that each side can do the same things. They learn to make the two sides work together to get a task done. This helps children develop an inner sense of the left and the right sides of themselves without necessarily being able to know left from right. Working in this Center, children learn their body position in space. They learn how far they are from objects and from others, moving toward, moving away, moving through the environments in which they find themselves. Activities that teach body awareness are valuable tools in enhancing a young child's development.

Eye-Hand Coordination

Eye-hand coordination is a critical skill. Children need their hands and their eyes to learn to work together. If they are to write, color, button, zip and cut they must be able to have the two working together accurately. The Motor Center provides many opportunities to develop this skill. Eye-foot coordination also is developed. This is necessary if children are to walk through the spaces and around the objects in their environment.

Visual Perception

Visual perception is enhanced in the Motor Center. When children learn to judge distance—how far, how close, how high—they are developing depth perception. This is important in going up and down stairs or sitting in a chair. Another facet of perception is visual discrimination. Children learn to discrimination between colors, shapes, sizes, symbols and other object characteristics that help them classify objects in the world. It allows them to group things and to capture them again through memory. Another component is figure-ground perception which children must develop to single out objects from cluttered backgrounds. Through involvement in motor activities and games, these skills develop in children naturally.

Creating the Motor Center

How can one create a Motor Center that has a good chance of accomplishing these things? The first consideration is space. A Motor Center takes up significant classroom space in the classroom. Children need to be able to move around freely. If you do not have space in the classroom, look around the school or building. A not-too-busy hallway, an empty stage or a small outdoor area might be an option. How about sharing an area with another classroom? Or rotating the Music Center with the Motor Center?

When you have found your space, organize it for independent activity. If you have a noncarpeted area, define the activity spaces with colored tape on the floor. If it is carpeted, define the boundaries with hook-sided, velcro strips (it sticks well to carpet without damaging it and it is easy to move boundaries). Remember, each activity needs its own space, because each one requires different amounts of space. For example the beanbag toss needs a long narrow area. The bats and balls need a larger, more square space for the activity. How many activities are out at one time depend on the space available and the number of children allowed in the space. Keep in mind that physical activities can be loud, potentially messy and generally busy and active, so place the Motor Center in a low traffic area.

Second, organize the activities themselves, so that all the components are together. To organize the beanbag toss, for example, put taped circles on the floor in the places where the containers will be kept. Mark the toss line with colored tape (or hook-sided velcro) 2' or 3' from the containers, and be prepared to move it when the children master tossing from the first toss line (the distance depends on the age and developmental level of the children). Have a basket or bucket for the beanbags so the children will know where to put them at clean up time. Put out a rebus (a picture direction) showing how the activity materials are to be used. Make sure the children can see it. When you put out the bats and balls, include a storage container. Look at each activity carefully. Think about how to make it self-directed and, as much as possible, how it can be organized for continuous use with minimum intervention by the teacher.

A challenging, physical program that is fun for children, fosters growth and development. Plan the area. Look at the safety aspects. Keep the area interesting and inviting. Be innovative. If you do this, children will be drawn to the Motor Center. Capitalize on children's natural desire to use their entire bodies to explore, learn and to express themselves.

Elastic Circles

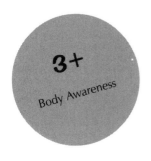

3+

Body Awareness

This is an easy and fun way to get children stretching and bending; moving creatively. They can work with a friend or alone.

Materials

✓ Chinese jump ropes or elastic, needles and thread
✓ basket
✓ paper
✓ markers

What to do

Purchase Chinese jump ropes or make elastic circles. To make the circles, purchase 5' lengths of 3/4" elastic; however, the exact length of the elastic you use will depend on the size of the children. So, measure it on the children before you sew the ends together.

Most of the children should be able to stand on the elastic with both feet and easily pull the elastic arms-length above their heads.

Use needle and thread and sew the ends together overlapping them 1".

The children use the circles by holding them in their hands and underneath their feet to make different shapes.

They put them behind them and stretch them in front of them.

They can lie down on the floor and stretch the circles from their heads to their feet.

Place the circles in the basket with the picture cards like those illustrated.

The children use the cards as a starting point in developing their own ideas as to how to use the elastic circles.

Note: If you want several children to work together, make the circle 15'-20' long.

Rope Exercises

3+

Language development
Body awareness

This activity gets children to use their large muscles and improves gross motor development. As children move, they will improve their sense of balance and their awareness of their bodies in space. The children need to follow directions in order to do the exercises, following the rebus or picture directions as they move from one exercise to the next.

Materials

✓ 6'-8' length of rope
✓ pictures of children hopping, walking, jumping, crawling
✓ self-adhesive paper or laminating film
✓ colored tape

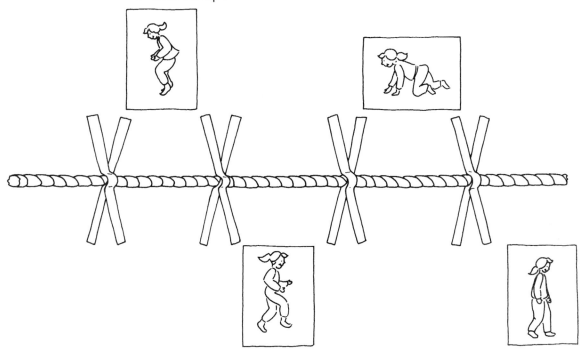

What to do

Find pictures, or draw them, of a child hopping, walking, jumping and crawling. Laminate the pictures or cover them with self-adhesive paper to extend their life.

Stretch the rope on the floor.

Mark off the activity area with colored tape allowing enough room on each side of the rope for the children to move from one end of the rope to the other.

Use colored tape to mark a large X on the floor at one end of the rope to designate a starting point.

Use tape to place the pictures along the length of the rope at 1' or 2' intervals.

When a child chooses this activity, she starts by standing on the X, she looks at the first picture, then duplicates the activity.

Next, she looks at the second picture, duplicates the exercise and she continues down the rope until all of the exercises are completed.

She can then choose to repeat the activity—standing in line, awaiting her turn—or move to another classroom area.

To make this more challenging, change the pictures to require more difficult movements or play follow the leader.

Ladder Walking

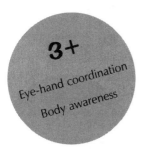

3+

Eye-hand coordination

Body awareness

Movement, coordination and balance play a large part in this activity. It encourages confidence in the child's own physical skills. In this activity, children are asked to imitate the movements and activities shown in magazine photographs and drawings or sketches. Use pictures that are appropriate for the skill level of the children.

Materials

✓ scissors
✓ paper
✓ colored tape
✓ magazines, catalogs, old books
✓ self-adhesive paper or laminating film
✓ construction
✓ glue
✓ wood rung ladder (not a step ladder)

What to do

Obtain a wood rung ladder (not a step ladder).

Find pictures in magazines, old books or catalogs of children walking and crawling.

Back the pictures with construction paper and laminate them to extend their life (or cover them with clear self-adhesive paper).

Cut out two shapes from construction paper to identify the starting place and the ending place.

Place the ladder on the floor in a space marked off with colored tape.

Place the ladder on the floor with the base at the starting point of the walk.

Put the pictures on the floor at different points, along the side of the ladder.

The child chooses the activity, starts the walk at the base of the ladder, walks along encountering the pictures and imitating the movements shown in them.

Balls and Bats

3+

Eye-hand coordination

Visual perception

It takes hand-eye coordination for children to hit a ball with a bat. For young children, make a wide bat and ball.

Materials

✓ purchased bat or coat hanger, stocking and tape
✓ purchased ball, pompom, or cardboard and yarn

What to do

Try making your own bats and balls. To make the bat, cover a coat hanger, that has been pulled into circular shape, with a stocking.

Tie the nonhook end in a knot.

Pull the other end tightly around the hook end of the coat hanger and tape it carefully.

Fold the hook closed (you will use it as a handle) and tape it well.

Use pompoms for the balls. To make them, wrap yarn around a 3″ piece of cardboard about 300 times.

Then cut one side free. Lay the pieces across a long piece of string.

Tie the string tightly around the yarn pieces. Trim the pieces to make a ball.

Note: Wadded up balls of newspaper work well, also.

Bat

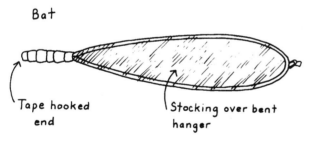

Tape hooked end

Stocking over bent hanger

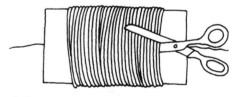

Cut yarn down middle.

Ball

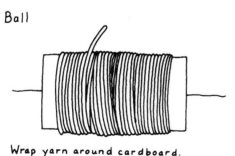

Wrap yarn around cardboard.

Tie string.

Leaf Play

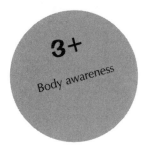

3+

Body awareness

This is an excellent activity for small children. They just love to jump, fall, scoop and toss in a pile of leaves.

Materials

✓ large bag of fall leaves
✓ small plastic swimming pool
✓ small broom and dust pan

What to do

Place the leaves in the pool.

Beside the pool place a small broom (child size) and a dust pan ready for the overflow of leaves that inevitably takes place.

The child plays in the leaf pool scooping up arms full of leaves, tossing them up and over her head, jumping in them, falling in them.

After a child is finished, she is responsible for cleaning up, sweeping up the leaves and returning them to the plastic pool.

Stompers

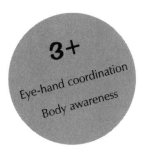

3+

Eye-hand coordination

Body awareness

This is a popular activity with children. It requires good balance and hand-foot-eye coordination.

Materials

✓ 2 coffee cans with lids (1-pound size)
✓ can opener (for teachers only)
✓ heavy-duty clothesline
✓ large basket

What to do

Make two holes in the coffee can, opposite one another, 1/2" from the rim of the closed end on the side of the can (use the puncturing-end of a can opener).

Cut two lengths of heavy-duty clothesline (the length will depend on the average height of the children).

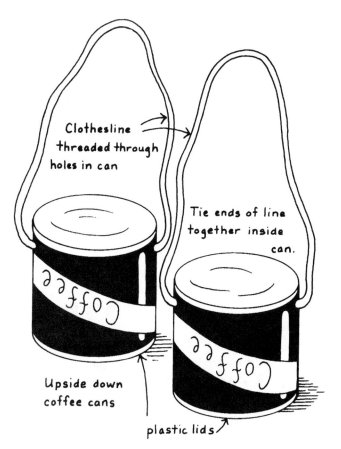

Clothesline threaded through holes in can

Tie ends of line together inside can.

Upside down coffee cans

plastic lids

Coffee

Coffee

Thread the strings through the holes on each side of the can and tie both of the ends together.

Place the plastic lids on the open end of the can.

Place the stompers in a large basket in a defined, carpeted space. When a child chooses the stompers, he gets two cans, pulls on the strings, tries to stand on the stompers, then walks, pulling on the strings as he moves his feet.

Box Play

3+

Eye-hand coordination
Visual perception

This activity gives the children a chance to crawl, climb, push and pull.

Materials

✓ large cardboard boxes
✓ hats (optional)
✓ props and accessories (optional)

What to do

Collect different sizes of cardboard boxes that are large enough for the children to get in.

Close down the other activities so there will be enough room for the children to organize the boxes in a variety of ways. They may make buses, airplanes, cars or trains.

After they have explored the boxes as they have configured them, give them accessories and props to use with the boxes. Collect hats of different kinds (fire fighters, police officers, auto racers, bus drivers) steering wheels and chairs. Props and accessories will change the style of play.

When the children are ready for a change, tape the boxes closed and cut holes large enough for them to crawl through the sides and tops of the boxes.

Obstacle Course

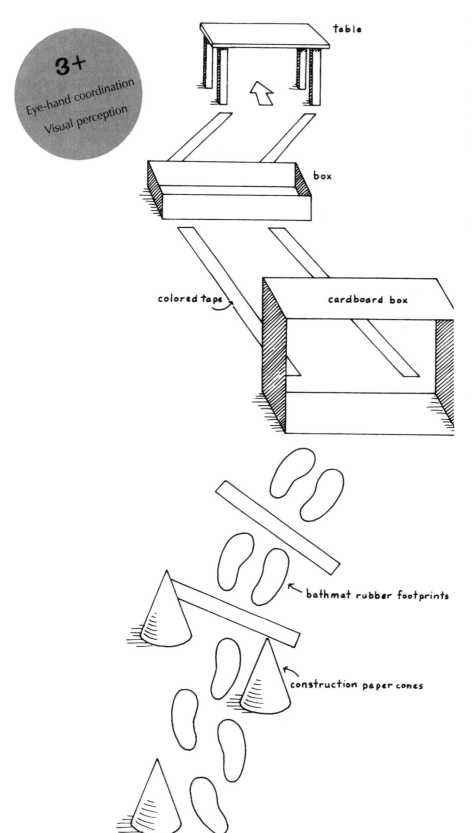

3+

Eye-hand coordination

Visual perception

table

box

colored tape

cardboard box

bathmat rubber footprints

construction paper cones

This can be as easy or as difficult as the children can manage. After the children understand the meaning of obstacle course, they can design some very challenging ones themselves for others to try.

Materials

✓ objects from the class room
✓ construction paper cones
✓ footprints cut out from old rubber bath or car mats
✓ tape
✓ colored tape or hula hoops
✓ large cardboard boxes

What to do

Use the equipment or objects that are available in the classroom. At first, use a simple design. Make it more complicated later.

Construct construction paper cones to mark off the spaces through the children are to walk, hop, run, roll, crawl.

Tape footprints on the floor. Make them by cutting footprint shapes from old rubber bath or car mats. Footprints are great for showing the children where to go and where to take giant steps.

Colored tape (or hook-sided velcro) or hula hoops on the floor further define the spaces in which the children are to move.

If possible, obtain a cardboard barrel from a natural food store and cut out both ends to make a tunnel.

Use large cardboard boxes for obstacles, for crawling through or for climbing in and out. For an example of a simple obstacle course, see the illustration.

Note: Be sure to sketch the obstacle course you make, enlarge it on the copy machine and post it on the wall beside the course. This is a great introduction to mapping. When the children design a course, make sure they make a sketch of it before they use it.

The Parachute Bounce

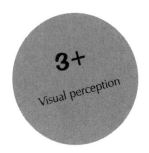

3+

Visual perception

This is a neat way to attract children who have not been interested in the Motor Center.

Materials

✓ old round tablecloth or king size sheet
✓ 5 or 6 soft balls, such as Nerf® balls

What to do

Make a parachute from a large, round, old tablecloth (sometimes parents can donate an old one) or cut one from an old king size sheet. It needs to be about 6' in diameter.

The parachute is small because classroom space is often limited.

This is a good size for four or five children to use at one time.

The children position themselves evenly around the edge of the parachute. They hold it taunt.

Each child tosses a soft ball into the middle of the parachute. The object is to bounce the balls as high as possible without having them fly off the parachute.

This activity can get very rowdy, so set up the activity area in a low traffic, out of the way area of the classroom or outside.

Note: There are many other fun things to do with the parachute. Encourage the children to create other games.

Beanbags and Cans

3+

Eye-hand coordination

Visual perception

Children love the challenge of trying to toss objects. As they practice, they develop more accuracy. This also can be a way to work toward numeral recognition and sets.

Materials

✓ 5 large coffee cans or cans the same size
✓ duct tape
✓ self-adhesive paper
✓ permanent marker
✓ colored tape
✓ 15 socks
✓ beans
✓ large basket

Throwline

What to do

Collect five large coffee cans or cans that are the same size. Make sure the metal rim is free of jagged edges or cover the edges with duct tape.

Cover the cans with self-adhesive paper.

Draw the numerals 1 through 5 on the front of each can and mark the corresponding number of dots on each can.

Make 15 bean bags. Use old white athletic socks with no holes in the toes.

Fill them from toe to heel with beans. Tie-off the sock or sew it closed.

Use a permanent marker to write the numeral: 1 on five of the socks; 2 on four of the socks; 3 on three of the socks; 4 on two of the socks; and 5 on one of the socks.

Put the corresponding number of dots on each sock.

Place the bean bags in a large basket. Affix a colored tape (or velcro) throw line to the floor and mark the location for the cans to be placed with colored tape (or velcro) on the floor.

The numbering scheme is only to allow the children to create their own games. Counting is not the object of this activity. There are many ways they can play. At first they may just toss the beanbags in the can. Later they may match the numbers. Later, some children may put the same number of beanbags in the can as the numeral written on the can. Some of the children may start keeping score, but this is up to the children. Provide no directions or goals other than to tell them to toss the beanbags in the cans. Let the children decide how they want to play.

Tennis Can Bowling

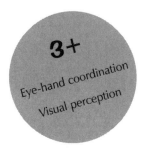

3+

Eye-hand coordination

Visual perception

This is an excellent way to have bowling indoors and have it be reasonably quiet while the children bend and stretch rolling a ball. It also reinforces math skills.

Materials

✓ 15 tennis cans with lids
✓ sand
✓ colored tape
✓ permanent marker
✓ medium-size soft ball, such as a Nerf® ball
✓ small basket
✓ paper and pencils

What to do

Put 1/2 cup of sand in each tennis can.

Put on the lids and tape them closed.

Use the permanent marker to write the numerals 1 to 15 on the cans.

Set up a bowling zone by using colored tape affixed to the floor to make an alley.

Put 15 Xs on the floor with colored tape in the shape of an equilateral triangle.

Place one can on each X.

Put a tape line (or hook-sided velcro) on the floor to mark the point from which the Nerf® ball is released.

Place the ball in a small basket near the bowling area.

Have paper and pencils nearby if the children decide to keep score. Let the children make up their own rules and their own method of score keeping.

When a child chooses this activity, he sets up the pins and rolls the ball. The activity can be done alone or with a friend.

Scoops and Balls

Children need opportunities to use the large muscles of the arm. Tossing and catching do this. It also teaches teamwork, coordination of one's effort with another.

Materials

✓ 4 plastic milk jugs
✓ 16 pairs of pantyhose
✓ scissors
✓ tape
✓ large container

What to do

Cut the milk jug into the shape of a scoop, following the illustration.

To make balls from the pantyhose, put three pairs of hose inside one pair pushing them down to the foot. Cut the stocking in two at mid-calf and stuff all of the remaining hose into the foot of the stocking. Tie-off the ball securely with the end of the stocking. Make four balls.

To prepare the area, tape off the toss and catch area.

Place the balls and scoops in a large container.

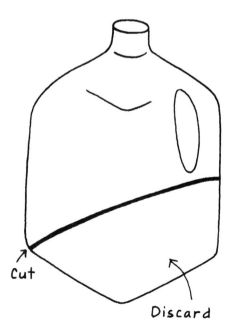

Cut

Discard

The major purpose of the activity is for the children to catch and toss the ball with the scoop. However, the children will invent a variety of games to play with the balls and scoops. They can toss the balls back and forth from scoop to scoop with a friend. They can play a form of hot-potato and toss the ball to another child quickly.

Ring Toss

3+

Eye-hand coordination

Visual perception

This is an excellent hand-eye coordination activity, one that will interest children.

Materials

✓ 10 to 12 long-neck, plastic salad dressing bottles
✓ sand
✓ markers
✓ rubber canning rings
✓ colored tape
✓ basket

What to do

Collect 10 or 12 long-neck, plastic salad dressing bottles. Remove the labels as they are being washed.

Fill each one to the top with sand and twist on the lid.

If the children have mastered numbers to the point that they are able to keep score, place numerals on each bottle.

To make tossing rings, purchase rubber canning jar rings or make tossing rings from empty masking tape rolls (to give them the necessary weight, cover them with colored tape).

Put colored tape Xs on the floor where the bottles are to be placed each time they are used. Put a colored tape line on the floor about 2' or 3' from the bottles to create a line from which the children toss the rings toward the bottles.

Place the rings in a basket next to the toss line.

When a child chooses this activity, he sets up the bottles on the Xs, gets the rings and tosses them one at a time toward the bottles.

He counts the number of rings that were caught on the bottles or the total points of the bottles that were ringed.

Cylinders and Balls

3+

Eye-hand coordination

Social development

Body awareness

Children learn through the challenge of working together with other children. This activity also is helpful in developing good hand-eye coordination.

Materials

✓ variety of cylinders
✓ variety of balls
✓ colored tape
✓ baskets

What to do

This activity works best when the children work in pairs.

Collect a variety of cylinders of different diameters and lengths. These can be obtained from the cardboard rolls such as paper towels, gift wrap, fabric, toilet paper, laminating film and other products.

Collect a variety of balls: ping-pong balls, whiffle balls, golf balls, tennis balls and other types of soft balls.

Mark off a play area with colored tape.

Place the cylinders in a large basket and put the balls in another.

Pair the children if they do not choose partners.

The children select cylinders and balls; one child rolls the balls down the cylinders, while the other child catches them.

The activity can be done by one child if a large bucket is placed at the open end of the cylinder into which the balls are rolled.

Beach Ball Play

3+

Eye-hand coordination

Visual perception

This will give the children an opportunity to work together cooperatively, as well as enhance their tossing and catching skills.

Materials

✓ 2 large coffee cans
✓ rocks
✓ 2 dowels (each 1 1/2' in diameter and 4' long)
✓ large beach ball
✓ 2 pieces of string (each 6' long)
✓ colored tape
✓ large container

What to do

To make the net for beach ball play, insert the dowels upright in the coffee cans and fill them with rocks.

Place the cans about 3' apart and tie a string across the top ends of the dowels.

Tie the second string two feet below the first.

Use colored tape to mark the play area.

Place the ball inside the play area in a large container. Have ample room on each side of the net so the children can chase the ball comfortably.

When children choose this activity they need to do so in pairs. They get the ball and toss it back and forth across the net to each other. The older children will create their own rules and develop a way to keep score.

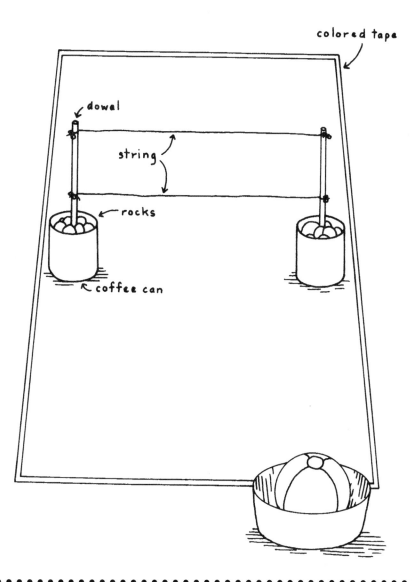

Balloon Play

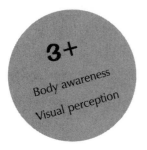

3+

Body awareness

Visual perception

Balloon play requires that children make large arm movements, the precursor to learning to use small muscles (large muscles develop first). If the activity is indoors encourage only arm movements, but when it is played outdoors running can be added.

Materials

✓ balloons
✓ crepe paper
✓ colored tape
✓ large basket

What to do

Blow up several balloons.

Attach a 2' long crepe paper streamer to each balloon.

Mark off a play area with colored tape.

Place the balloons in a large basket.

The child chooses the activity, selects a balloon from the basket and ties the streamer to her wrist (or she asks a friend to tie it). She swings her arm forward to make the balloon move upward, then she attempts to hit the balloon with the same hand to which the streamer and balloon are attached. For younger children allow them to hit the balloon with the other hand. For older children make the crepe paper streamer longer to make it more challenging.

Wax Paper Ice Skating

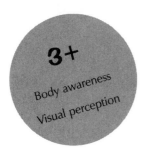

3+

Body awareness

Visual perception

In some parts of the United States it does not get very cold in the winter. For those living in these warm climates there is not much of an opportunity for outdoor winter sports, like ice skating. This activity offers a reasonable indoor substitute, enhanced by children's active imagination and their willingness to try new things. Wax paper skating requires good muscle control, so offer it to older children who are developmentally able. Limit the number of skaters at one time to two or three. Wax paper skating works best on a hard surface floor, but it can be done on carpeting if you think the children are just a little too young to attempt it on a hard surface.

Materials

✓ wax paper
✓ scissors
✓ rubber bands
✓ colored tape
✓ basket

What to do

Cut wax paper into 2' squares.

Mark off the skating area with colored tape.

Place the sheets of wax paper in a basket and the rubber bands in a container close to the basket.

When a child chooses this activity, he gets two pieces of wax paper and puts them on the bottom of each foot.

He uses the rubber bands to attach the wax paper around his ankles. He must make sure that the bottoms of his feet are covered.

He skates on the wax paper inside the defined boundaries.

Note: This is a very slippery activity, so keep safety in mind at all times. You might want to turn on the air conditioner and have caps and scarves handy to enhance the winter mood. Play "Skaters Waltz" and have the children skate to the music.

Loop-A-Stick

4+

Eye-hand coordination

Visual perception

Children find this activity challenging and they will work tirelessly trying to make it work.

Materials

✓ cardboard cylinder rods
✓ rubber canning jar rings
✓ string
✓ hole punch

What to do

Collect several cardboard cylinder rods (they come on coat hangers that dry cleaners use to hand slacks) and rubber canning jar rings (you can purchase the rings in a store that sells home canning supplies).

Thread a 3 1/2' length of string through the rod.

Tie-off one end of the string to one end of the rod (the rods are already slit, so use the slit to tie-off one end of the string).

Use a hole punch and make a hole in the protruding flap on the round rubber ring.

Thread the other end of the string through the hole.

Place the loop-a-stick in a container in a defined space in the Center.

The child selecting this activity will hold one end of the rod and try to swing the loop over the other end.

Note: If you cannot find the sealing rings, try using soft plastic flexible children's bracelets.

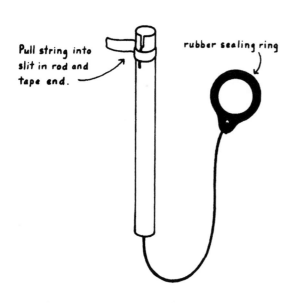

Pull string into slit in rod and tape end.

rubber sealing ring

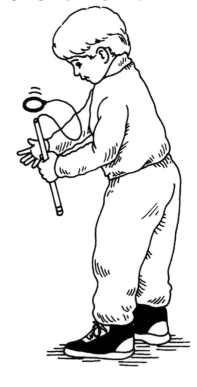

Ball Catch

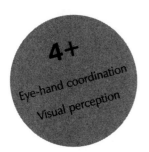

4+

Eye-hand coordination

Visual perception

This is a different version of Loop-A-Stick (see page 161). It involves more use of the large muscle groups in the arms and shoulders.

Materials

✓ toilet plunger
✓ soft ball, such as Nerf® ball
✓ string
✓ large-eye needle

What to do

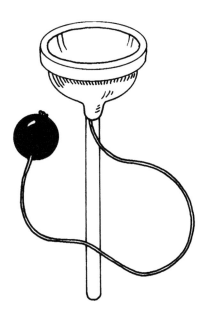

Purchase a short handle toilet plunger and a small soft ball.

Remove the plunger head.

Use a 3″ large-eye needle to thread a 3′ length of string through the middle of the ball.

Tie-off the string using a large knot.

Remove the needle.

Tie the opposite end of the string to the screw end of the plunger handle.

Now, screw the handle into the plunger head.

Put the ball catch in a container in a defined space in the Center.

When a child chooses the activity, she swings the ball, trying to catch it with the plunger cup.

A special thank you to Dianne Jurek for this idea.

Plunger Pull

4+

Social development

Body awareness

This not only requires the use of large muscles but it requires some problem solving skills and social skills working together with others. The activity typically is noisy, but the children have a great time with it.

Materials

✓ 2 short handle plungers
✓ container

What to do

Purchase two short handled plungers.

Place them in a container in a defined space in the Center.

The children pair up with a partner, get the two plungers and push them together until they create a vacuum; then, they try to pull them apart.

Chapter 8

The Music Center

Children and music are a natural combination. A child will burst spontaneously into song just to hear her own voice and express her feelings at the moment. As a child sings a song or moves to a beat, she is exploring and practicing important developmental skills. Since movement is an essential and natural part of the music it should be accommodated in the Music Center.

Language development

Music is a special language, written in a unique way, but exposure to music encourages language development generally. If children can write or pretend to write their own music on blank music sheets, they are learning to write and to read. Listening skills are developed when children use tapes or records of songs to be learned or instrumental music to be enjoyed.

Math

As children sing, they accomplish a number of things. They develop new vocabulary words and they practice old ones. They practice the articulation and the pronunciation of words. One of the foundations of math and reading is being able to create, recognize and repeat patterns. Since music is patterns, every song a child sings, every song a child creates, every clapping, tapping and stomping to music is a pattern experienced. To learn the songs to sing, a child must recognize sounds and to compare them. This comparison is performed below the level of their awareness—it just happens! Musical patterns—notes, rhythms, beats and tones—require similarities and differences discrimination, an important developmental task. As this occurs, a child actually can hear the rhyming words that occur in music. This is another important reading and math skill.

Motor Development

As a child sings and moves, she is feeling the meaning of the music and growing control she has over her body. When children move or dance with each other, they develop social skills while working in harmony with others. As children clap, tap and snap their fingers, they practice control of small muscle groups. When they pantomime movement to music and act out a song, children develop nonverbal communication skills.

Science

Science occurs naturally in this Center. When a child strikes a triangle she discovers cause and effect: If I do this, then that happens. When a child plays a xylophone she finds out about pitch and she feels the sound waves passing upward through her fingers, hand and arms, and resonating in her ears. She learns about sound and volume (and how soft and loud effect her and others). As she dances and jumps to music she feels her weight pulling against the forces of gravity.

Creating the Music Center

How can a teacher set up a Music Center in a way that works for young children? First is the deciding where to put the center. It needs to be in an area where there is space for movement and for dancing. Electrical outlets for the record player and tape recorder are necessary. It should be located in the noisier part of the classroom.

You will need shelving to contain the musical instruments. You usually have about ten instruments at a time so the shelf needs to be fairly large. Put silhouettes of the instruments on the shelf to indicate where the instruments are kept when not being used. Another way to display the instrument choice is to use pictures attached to baskets. Place each instrument and a picture of it in individual baskets on the shelves. Either way, there needs to be a defined space for each instrument being used. Usually displaying one of each type or set of instruments on the shelf at a time is sufficient. Rotate the instruments when interest in any particular instrument wanes.

Another shelf is necessary to hold the activities that will be available for choice by the children. These activities also need to be in a basket, tub or tray. Change the activities as interest wanes. Use this shelf for other props like a drum major's hat, a conductor's baton, a cheerleader's pompom and a megaphone. You might want to add a stuffed animal that goes with a particular song like a spider on a string to go with the "Eensy, Weensey Spider." A cardboard box car could be put in the Center to go with "The Little Girl in the Car." The children use these props to dramatize the songs. Books that show the songs written on musical staffs, storybooks about children, and music and musical instruments are other good additions to these shelves. Add a folder with blank sheet music and pencils for writing music.

A small table for the record player and tape recorder, easily accessible to the children, is a critical part of this Center. Leave out a selection of records and tapes that they can use freely. Put each in a container. Be sure to include a variety of music, not just children's songs. There will be one type of music that attracts a particular child who never chooses to come to the Center. Copy the records that you do not want damaged onto tapes. Store these "not for children's use" records out of reach. Make copies of the tapes the children use so that damaged tapes can be replaced. Put rebuses (picture directions) on the wall close by to explain how to use the tape recorder and the record player.

It would be best if the teacher had a record player for her own use and the children had another one. Look for old record players at a flea market or garage sale. Let the children use this one. Keep the good record player in a place that is out of reach to the children but accessible to you.

Mark off the dancing and movement area with a colored tape line (or hook-sided velcro) allowing plenty of room. If colored tape is not a good choice and velcro does not work because of the floor material, try making a chalk line. It is easy to erase, making change in the center easy.

Set up the Music Center for self-directed play that will require little or no supervision. Many children may spend all of their center time in this Center. This is good since so many of the skills and concepts young children need to develop are available in the Center. Reading, writing, language development, physical development as well as creative expression happen in a well prepared environment. There is no need to hurry a child or encourage him to work in another area if you have equipped and organized the Center as discussed.

Ribbon Dancing

3+

Language & Motor development

Movement, motion, dancing and singing are big interests of children.

Materials

✓ pieces of cloth ribbon in 3'-4' lengths
✓ 1/2" diameter dowel, cut into 8"-12" lengths
✓ eye hooks
✓ notebook rings
✓ hot glue gun

What to do

Make a ribbon stick by attaching a cloth ribbon to a dowel.

Screw an eye hook into one end of the dowel. One way to create a ribbon stick is to simply tie the ribbon onto the eye hook.

To make it a bit longer lasting try a more complicated approach. Attach the ribbon to a notebook ring by folding it over the curve of the ring and using a hot glue gun to seal it.

Then close the ring into the eye hook. This keeps the ribbon from being knotted as the children use it. Either way, the children use the ribbon to move to music.

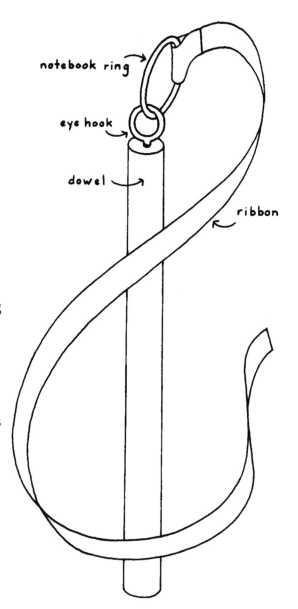

Bag Dancing

Some children are reluctant to express themselves in dance. The following activity is perfect for those children.

Materials

✓ see-through old laundry bag
✓ marker

What to do

Take an old laundry bag and draw a large face on it.

The child puts the bag over her head and dances in the bag to music. The child can see through the laundry bag so she will not hurt herself.

Note: Use a large laundry bag; a pillowcase is too small for the children to move their arms and children cannot see through a pillowcase.

Streamers

Movement is used by children and adults to express moods and emotions. The following activity invites children to use their arms enthusiastically while developing large muscles and expressing feelings.

Materials

✓ coat hanger
✓ glue
✓ 20" long crepe paper streamers
✓ tape

What to do

Bend the coat hanger into a circular shape.

Fold up the hanger end and tape it carefully.

Cut 20 crepe paper streamers, each 20" long.

Glue them around the circular shape, turn on some lively music and watch the show as the children take turns interpreting what they hear.

Note: Save leftover laminating film and cut it into 2" x 15" strips and tape them around the coat hanger circle as above. Use this during a winter study. The film makes an icy sound.

Scarf Dancing

3+

Language & Motor development

This is a good way to get the children to start moving to music. Giving children props helps them overcome their inhibitions to dance in front of others. They use the scarves to help them dramatize the sounds they hear.

Materials

✓ lightweight scarves
✓ basket
✓ picture of child dancing with scarves

What to do

Collect lightweight scarves of all colors. Chiffon scarves work the best. They allow the children to be so much more expressive. Chiffon is light and it floats in the air. Look at a flea market, garage sale or a dime store to find them.

Place the scarves in a basket on the music shelf along with a rebus (picture direction) showing a child dancing with the scarves.

When a child chooses the basket, he reads the rebus and dances with the scarves.

Mirror Dancing

3+

Motor & Social development

Dance is more than artistic expression—interpretation and physical movement—it offers younger children a chance to become aware of their own movement in a world of objects and of others.

Materials

✓ none needed

What to do

This activity requires no props, just pairs of children.

Place two children in front of each other. One is the mirror, the other is the dancer.

The child who is the mirror reproduces the movements of the dancing child.

Encourage them to mirror dance to both fast music and slow music.

Encourage them to change roles.

Leaves

3+

Language development

Math

This activity is a fun way to practice counting. It also encourages the children to use their listening skills.

Materials

✓ 9 fall leaves, real or artificial
✓ 9 pieces of ribbon, string or yarn (each 10" long)
✓ hot glue gun
✓ basket

What to do

Use a hot glue gun to attach the ribbons to the leaves.

Teach the children the song below.

Select nine children to hold the leaves; assign each child a number.

They drop the leaves when they sing their number.

LEAVES ARE FALLING by Sharon MacDonald

(tune: "Are You Sleeping")

Leaves are falling.

One, two, three.

From the tree.

Four, five, six.

Falling to the ground.

Seven, eight, nine.

Leaves are falling down.

Covering the ground.

When the children understand how to do the activity and they have learned the song, place the leaves in a basket on the music shelf. The children who want to do the activity can do it over and over.

Tennis Racket Guitar

Using pretend musical instruments are as much fun as real ones. It also helps move the children from the real to the representational, an important step in reading.

Materials

✓ old tennis racket or racquetball racket
✓ ribbon

What to do

Make a guitar by taking an old tennis racket or racquetball racket and tie a ribbon from the frame around the racket head to the racket handle.

The child puts the racket around her neck and immediately becomes a rock star.

Add a bale of hay to the Center and a cowpoke's hat and the child becomes a country and western star.

A special thanks to Sharron Lucky for this idea.

Kitchen Band

Another way for children to represent real instruments using pretend instruments is to create a pots and pans band.

Materials

✓ kitchen pots, pans, spoons

What to do

Collect wooden spoons, metal pots with lids of different sizes, skillets and pans of different depths.

The children strike the lids with the wooden spoon, strike the lids against the pots and clap the lids together.

Turn the pots over and have the children use a whisk broom for a soft, mellow sound. You can also use a wire whisk to slide around inside the pans.

Note: Use old pots and pans.

Bell Bracelet

3+

Language development

Science

By having opportunities to play with rhythm instruments, children become aware of timbre, pitch and volume. In this activity children will help make bracelets to use when dancing to music.

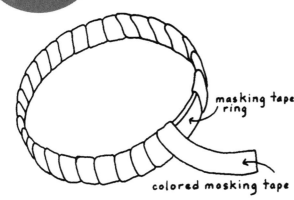

masking tape ring

colored masking tape

Materials

✓ empty masking tape rolls
✓ several sizes of jingle bells
✓ colored masking tape
✓ ice pick (for teachers only)
✓ elastic thread
✓ scissors
✓ basket

What to do

Wrap the empty tape rolls with colored masking tape.

Use an ice pick to make two holes, 1/2" apart.

Move around the circumference 1 1/2" and make two more holes 1/2" apart. Do this a total of three times. This will leave about half of the roll without holes. The children can hold onto this half if they choose not to wear the roll as a bracelet.

Cut six lengths of elastic, each 4" long.

Tie a bell in the center of the thread.

Thread the two ends of the thread into two of the holes on the roll that are 1/2" apart and tie the ends inside the roll. Repeat this procedure for each set of holes until there are three jingle bells on each cylinder. Mix the size of the bells on each bracelet or make the bells on each bracelet the same size.

Place the bracelets in a basket on the music shelf. When a child chooses the bell basket, she puts on the bracelet and jingles them to music or song.

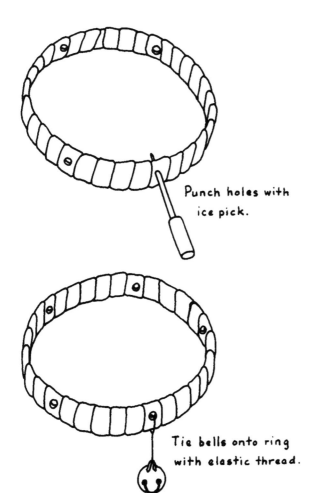

Punch holes with ice pick.

Tie bells onto ring with elastic thread.

Kazoo

3+

Motor development

Science

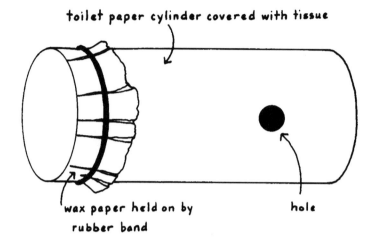

toilet paper cylinder covered with tissue

wax paper held on by
rubber band

hole

Children enjoy making their own musical instruments. They can use the idea at home and make the kazoo over and over again. This also teaches recycling.

Materials

✓ 1 toilet paper cylinder for each child
✓ wax paper circles cut 5″ in diameter
✓ small rubber bands
✓ pieces of tissue paper cut to fit around the cylinders
✓ scissors

What to do

The children cover the cylinders with the tissue paper.

They put the wax paper circles over one end of the cylinder and put the rubber band over it to hold it on the cylinder.

The teacher uses the sharp end of the scissors to make a hole in the middle of the cylinder.

The children hum into the open end of the cylinder to make music.

Tea Strainer Shakers

3+

Language development

Science

Young children enjoy creating and discovering new sounds. This encourages a child to listen while trying to discriminate between sounds.

Materials

✓ tea strainers
✓ pebbles, rice, beans, paper clips
✓ tape
✓ small basket

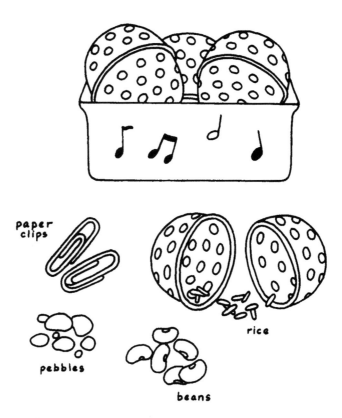

What to do

Purchase different size tea strainers.

Put pebbles in one tea strainer, rice in one, beans in one and paper clips in the last one. Screw tightly or tape closed.

Place the shakers in a small basket on the music shelf along with a rebus (picture direction) showing a child shaking the shakers.

The children choose the shakers to create music or to play along with a record or tape.

Egg Shakers

3+

Language development

Science

This is another fun shaker activity. The sound created by shaking each shaker is different, so it gives the children a chance to compare sounds.

Materials

✓ stocking containers (type that have one or both sides of the container made of clear plastic)
✓ buttons, sand, sequins, small corks
✓ tape
✓ basket

What to do

Put buttons in one container, sand in another, sequins in another and small corks in another.

Tape them together around the middle.

Place the shakers in a basket on the music shelf along with a rebus (picture direction).

The children use the shakers to make music or to play along with a record or tape.

Note: If you cannot find stocking containers, use clear Christmas ornaments that are used to make hanging decorations for the tree. You can find these in a craft store.

Horseshoe Triangle

3+

Language development

Science

Children are able to use and to appreciate the subtleties and complexities of sound as they grow and develop. Therefore, their ability to differentiate sounds grows from simple to complex.

Materials

✓ old horseshoe
✓ large heavy-duty rubber band
✓ 10" nail
✓ basket

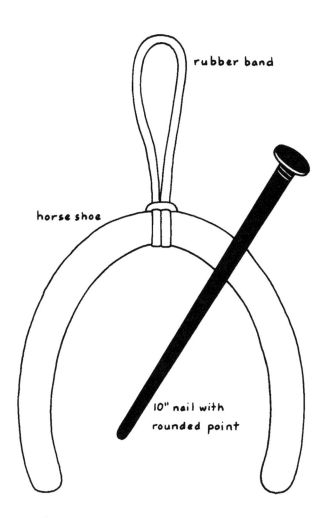

rubber band

horse shoe

10" nail with
rounded point

What to do

Find an old horseshoe, a large, heavy-duty rubber band and a 10" nail.

Place the rubber band on the horseshoe.

File off the pointed end of the nail.

Place the horseshoe and the nail in a basket on the music shelf. The children use the nail to strike the triangle while holding it by the rubber band that allows it to hang freely so it will vibrate when struck.

Encourage the children to compare the sound of the horseshoe triangle to the regular triangle. Talk about the sound made by each triangle.

In and Out Box

• •

3+

Language & Motor development

Through creative movement, children learn that all movement is not dancing. Large muscle development is encouraged through this activity.

Materials

✓ large cardboard box
✓ scissors

What to do

Find a cardboard box large enough for a child to get into, such as a TV box or refrigerator box.

Cut out a large hole on the top and one in each of the four vertical sides.

Cut the holes large enough for a child to stick out his head and shoulders.

As music is played, a child moves to the music in the box: up and down, in and out of the holes.

• •

Hub Cap Drum

3+

Language development

Science

Musical instruments offer children a variety of ways to experiment with sounds and to create new ones.

Materials

✓ old metal hub cap
✓ wooden spoons
✓ tray

What to do

Find an old metal hub cap and collect a couple of wooden spoons. Place the hub cap drum and spoons on a tray on the music shelf along with a rebus (picture direction) showing the children how to use the activity.

The children use the spoons to strike the hub cap.

Bicycle Horn Band

3+

Language development

Math

These are wonderful sound makers to add to your collection of rhythm instruments. The children can compare the different sounds coming from the horns.

Materials

✓ bicycle horns
✓ tray

What to do

Collect a variety of bicycle horns. Be sure to get plastic horns as well as metal ones, short as well as long ones, crooked as well as straight ones.

Place the horns on a tray on the music shelf along with a rebus showing the children how to use the activity.

The children use the horns to create a new and interesting sound and sound combinations. This is an opportunity for children to work together to make music.

Balloon Dancing

3+

Language & Motor development

This activity is best done outside where there is lots of space.

Materials

✓ balloons
✓ 2' long crepe paper streamers
✓ recorded music

What to do

Tie balloons of different colors to crepe paper streamers, one for each child.

Tie the streamers to each child's wrist.

Take a record or tape player outside and play music for dancing. It really becomes exciting if you choose a windy day.

Note: If you want to set this up as a self-directed activity in the classroom, put out two balloons for two children to use at the same time. Close other Music Center activities for the day.

Flower Pot Music

3+

Language development Math & Science

This activity offers the children a chance to become more proficient in their sound making abilities. Soon, they will be able to analyze the differences in the sound they produce.

Materials

✓ clay flower pots   ✓ wooden spoon
✓ string   ✓ notebook rings
✓ chart stand or other place from which to hang the pots

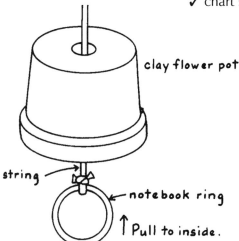

clay flower pot

string

notebook ring

↑ Pull to inside.

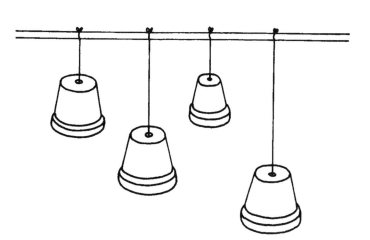

What to do

Collect clay flower pots with a hole in each of the pot bottoms. Use four or five different sizes.

Thread a piece of string through the inverted bottom of the pot and attach it to a notebook ring placed inside the pot.

Tie all of the pots to the top of the chart stand (or hang from another place in the classroom).

Hang the pots at different lengths, so that when they are struck by the children with the wooden spoon, they will not swing and hit each other.

When a child chooses the activity, he strikes the different pots with the wooden spoon to make music.

Cylinder Board

3+
Language development
Math & Science

The following activity shows the children a way to recycle. It also enhances their listening skills as each cylinder makes a different sound.

Materials

✓ cardboard cylinders
✓ self-adhesive paper
✓ wooden spoons
✓ 12" x 24" piece of cardboard
✓ glue
✓ tray

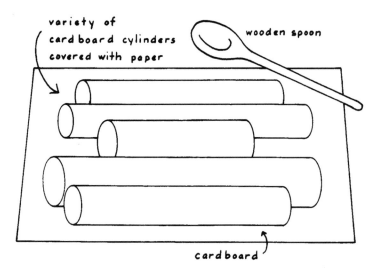

variety of cardboard cylinders covered with paper

wooden spoon

cardboard

What to do

Collect six or seven cardboard cylinders of different diameters, length and thickness. For example, toilet paper cylinder, paper towel cylinder, a cylinder that upholstery fabrics come on, a gift wrap paper cylinder.

Cover each cylinder with decorative self-adhesive paper.

Glue the cylinders side to side and then glue them to the cardboard piece. The cylinders should run lengthwise on the cardboard. Place the cylinder board and the spoon on a tray on the music shelf along with a rebus (picture direction) showing the children how to use the activity.

The children use the spoon to drag back and forth across the cylinders creating musical sounds. They can use it to play a song or with a tape or a record.

Washboard Music

3+

Language & Motor development

This offers the children a chance to experiment with the different sounds that can be made with an improvised musical instrument.

Materials

✓ small washboard
✓ thimbles
✓ basket

What to do

Purchase a small washboard. These can be found in a craft store or at flea markets.

Find several thimbles. Place one thimble in a small container beside the washboard on the music shelf. Put the other thimbles away to replace lost thimbles.

You may want to copy the illustration below and put it in the basket with the activity to show the children how to use the equipment. The children put the thimble on their finger or thumb, and rub it up and down on the washboard making music and experimenting with the different sounds that can be made. They might be familiar with the zydeco music washboard sound.

Children can learn to play music together by using the washboard with bicycle horns (see page 178).

Bass Instrument

4+

Language & Physical development

Make a simple and inexpensive string bass instrument that will provide a unique experience in sound that children can explore.

Materials

✓ round oatmeal container
✓ 2 notebook rings
✓ self-adhesive paper
✓ 4' length of fishing line
✓ ice pick (for teachers only)

What to do

Cover the oatmeal container with self-adhesive paper.

Remove the lid and use the ice pick to make a hole in the bottom of the container.

Thread the fishing line through the hole in the bottom of the container and tie it to a notebook ring inside the container.

Leave the ring inside the container and replace the lid.

Turn the container upside down. The string should come out of the hole in the bottom.

Tie the second notebook ring to the other end of the fishing line.

The child plays the bass instrument by placing it on the floor and pulling the string taunt by the notebook ring.

The child puts a foot on the container beside the string, holds the string by one hand and plucks the fishing line with the other. The bass instrument is used to make music or to accompany a song. The children learn that they can change the pitch of the bass by pulling the fishing line tighter or by releasing the tension on the string.

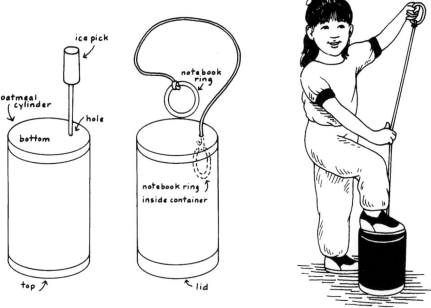

Wind-Up Toy

4+

Language & Motor development

Children are more free to express themselves when they are invited to pretend. This activity asks them to play like a wind-up toy.

Materials

✓ toilet paper cylinder
✓ cardboard
✓ aluminum foil
✓ scissors
✓ basket

What to do

Cut the cylinder in half. Throw one half away.

Cover the remaining half with aluminum foil.

Cut two slits in one end of the covered cylinder, one at the nine o'clock position and the other at the three o'clock position. Cut the slits about 1" deep into the body of the cylinder.

Design a key shape with a 1" insertion flap from the cardboard piece (the flap will be inserted into the slits on the end of the cylinder).

Cover the key head and the flap with aluminum foil. Insert the flap into the slits on the end of the cylinder. It is now a magic key that turns children into wind-up toys.

Put the key in a basket on the music shelf. When the children choose it, they need to find a friend to wind-up. Put on different types of music for the toy to dance to.

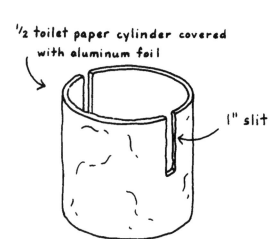

½ toilet paper cylinder covered with aluminum foil

1" slit

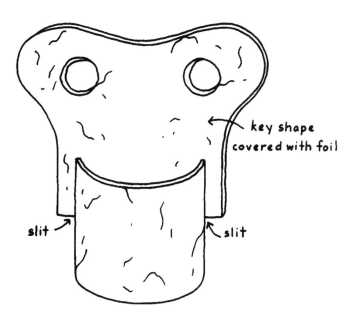

key shape covered with foil

slit

slit

Nail Tapping

4+

Language development

Math & Science

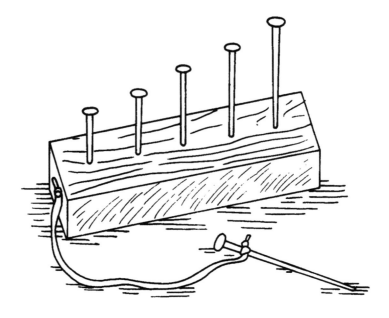

This activity helps children practice auditory discrimination skills. Which sounds high, low and in between?

Materials

✓ 4 or 5 large nails (each 8"-14" long)
✓ sand paper
✓ block of wood, 3"-4" thick
✓ hammer
✓ 54" (or longer) shoe string
✓ small nail

What to do

File the point of the longest nail; it will be used as the striker. Hammer the other nails into the block of wood about 3" apart moving from the shortest to the longest and from left to right.

Drive the nails 2" into the wood block so the children cannot pull them out.

Tie a 54" shoe string around the striker nail.

Nail the other end of the shoe string to one end of the block of wood with a small nail. This allows the children to use the striker to strike the different size nails but it limits the range the children can swing the nail.

The children strike the nails in any order to see which is higher in pitch, lower and in between.

Cup Tapping

4+
Language development
Math & Science

This following activity is another way to encourage creating, extending, recognizing and repeating patterns by tapping cups together to music.

Materials

✓ 2 plastic cups for each child
✓ basket

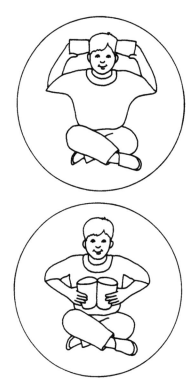

What to do

This is a good activity to introduce during group music time. At first, model a tapping pattern to the song on the next page, using the cups and tapping them together. Be creative! The children copy your tapping pattern.

Allow a child to create one for everybody to use. When the children understand the concept and they demonstrate that they know how to do the activity, place the cups in a basket on the music shelf.

This will give the children a starting point for making up their own tapping patterns to go with the song.

Along with the cups, include pattern cards (see illustrations). Copy the pattern cards or make you own.

Laminate or cover the cards with clear self-adhesive plastic to make them more durable.

Put out only enough cups for the number of children that can work comfortably in the Music Center.

If the children using the Center choose this activity, they can repeat your pattern with the cups or create their own using the pattern cards. Allow children to pair up, share and duplicate each other's patterns.

TAPPING SONG by Sharon MacDonald

(tune: "My Name Is Stegosaurus")

These cups are made for tapping.

It's a funny little game I play.

I tap them here, I tap them there.

Come play my funny game this way.

Tap in and out and in and out.

Tap down and down and down.

Tap over, under, on your head.

Tap all your body round.

Note: If you do not know the tune, just make up one or use the words as a chant.

Chapter 9

The Pouring Center

The Pouring Center is an exciting and inviting place for young children. Children come to school with different skills, abilities, interests and needs; yet, virtually all children are drawn to open-ended exploration of the different materials and tasks presented at the Pouring Center.

Language Development

Children learn to name the object, express actions, see relationships and to convey thoughts with words. More complete verbal expression is elicited from the activities themselves. The value is evident in that the more the Center is used the more the children learn and express, reaching for the words; learning from other children who are further along in the process of word use and the complex process of thought-action description.

Math and Science

Unbeknownst to the children, while the Pouring Center invites them to develop fine motor skills, they are also working with concepts like more/less, full/empty, liquid/solid and hard/soft. They experiment with the properties of different materials, observing similarities and differences. Children also develop problem solving skills while learning to pour and scoop. For example, a child might say to herself, "If I pour four scoops in the container, it spills over the sides. How many scoops are needed just to fill it? Three plus a little more?"

Motor Development

Scooping, pouring, dripping, mixing, measuring and stirring are safe and immediate opportunities for children to experience success.

Creating the Pouring Center

How can a teacher develop and set up an effective Pouring Center? It can be a part of the Discovery (Science) Center or it can stand alone, depending on the space you have in your room. Locate the Center away from high traffic areas.

Having a water or sand table for the pouring activities is ideal. Another way to create a Pouring Center is to place a large baby bath tub or a dish pan in the Center for the pouring activities. Limit the number of children using the Center to the number of children that comfortably can work at the size of the container chosen. For example, two children could play at a baby bath tub; a dishpan, on the other hand, because it is smaller, might allow for only one child. More children require more places to work. You might consider having two or three dishpans with the same activities in each to accommodate more children.

A way to define the work space for children is to put large Xs on the floor using colored tape. If the floor space is carpeted, use hook-sided velcro strips to make the Xs. The X shows the child where he is to work and it also helps control the number of children in the Center. When there is a child on each X, the Center is full.

Helpful tips to make the center more manageable and child-directed.

If the material being used in the Center is liquid, have plastic smocks for each child on nearby hooks. Have the children get their own smocks, put them on and return them to the hooks when they are through. A mop and a towel are also useful.

If the material is solid, like sand, have a small whisk broom, a dust pan and a trash can close by for the children to clean up spills.

Change the materials in the Center when you notice the children are losing interest. For instance, if you have sand at the table and the children are not choosing the Center, put the sand away. Substitute a cornstarch colloid. Reintroduce the sand later. Children enjoy variety. When they are tired of a material, they may begin to misuse it. It is then time to change and renew their interest.

Place the center as close to a water source as possible. This is not only useful when you have water in the Center, but also when you clean the table or change materials.

If you want the accessory equipment like the scoops, cups, bowls, removed from the table on a daily basis, provide a bucket or large container for this equipment storage. Ask the children to place the equipment in the bucket when they are through with the activity. If water was used, provide a sieve-like container and a bucket so the wet equipment can drain without dripping on the floor. The children can do much for themselves if you establish this expectation at the outset.

Use rebuses (step-by-step picture directions) as much as possible. They show the children how to use the various materials and equipment properly. These simply drawn pictures invite the children to read along and to work at their own pace. Many of the illustrations that accompany the activities in this book can be easily converted into rebuses by adding the written directions to the pictures. Consider the ability level of the children when adding the words.

A Pouring Center which has rebuses is like having a second teacher in the classroom. The children become so completely involved in what they are doing that often they are not aware of the passage of time and of the presence of others in the classroom. Give this Center a try. Teach the children to use it properly, and you will be glad you made this addition to your classroom.

Pouring

3+

Motor development

Math & Science

Water is the most popular activity in the Pouring Center.

Materials

✓ water table, baby bath tub or dish pans
✓ water
✓ liquid detergent
✓ blue food coloring (optional)
✓ plastic measuring cups, ladles, scoops

What to do

Fill the tub or table one-quarter to one-third full of water.

Add a drop or two of liquid detergent to help keep it clean.

Add a drop or two of blue food coloring if desired.

For the first experience with water keep the materials simple. Provide plastic measuring cups of various sizes and ladles of various sizes. The long handles of ladles are easier for the children to manage. If you cannot find ladles, use scoops instead.

Soapy Water

3+

Motor development

Math & Science

Not only is water popular with teachers but it is a favorite of children. They will spend hours playing with it (even longer if you add soap).

Materials

✓ water table, baby bath tub or dish pans
✓ liquid detergent
✓ plastic measuring cups and utensils
✓ straws
✓ scissors
✓ paper towels

What to do

Fill the tub or table one-quarter full of water.

Pour in 1/4 cup of liquid detergent. As the children pour, scoop, drip and dribble, the soap bubbles appear.

When they have created enough bubbles, put away the equipment they were using and add straws.

The children will use the straws to blow into the soapy water. However, if the children are "suckers" rather than "blowers," sidestep a potential problem by cutting a small opening, about one-third the way down from the top of each straw, so that the children cannot suck up the soap. They can still suck, but they will not be able to suck the soapy water into their mouths.

Have the children use the straws to blow into the soapy water and watch the bubbles appear. Some of the bubbles will be launched from the surface to the children's delight. (By the way, you might want to do this outside so the children can chase their floating bubbles.)

Keep a roll of paper towels close by for clean up.

Washing the Baby

3+

Language, Motor & Social development

Children love to imitate adult roles. Use the Pouring Center to provide an opportunity for them to do this.

Materials

✓ water table, baby bath tub or dish pans
✓ towel
✓ soap
✓ sponge
✓ wash cloth
✓ small towel
✓ baby dolls

What to do

Fill the tub or table one-third full with water.

Cover a small table with a towel and place it near the water table.

Place at the table: a bar of soap, a sponge, a wash cloth and a small towel for each child using the Center.

Give each child a baby doll to bathe.

Additional things to wash include: doll clothes, dishes or plastic toys.

Moving Water With Sponges

3+

Motor development

Math & Science

Sponges, water and children are a delightful combination. Squeezing sponges is a starting point for the children to develop and control the muscles of the hand.

Materials

✓ water table, baby bath tub or dish pans
✓ 2 small buckets
✓ large sponge

What to do

Place the two small buckets or containers in the table or tub.

Fill one with water.

Give the children a large sponge that fits easily into each container.

Have the children move the water from one container to the other by soaking up the water in one container and then squeezing it into the other.

The children quickly learn that the sponge will hold only a certain amount of water and no more.

If you have a variety of sponges the children can compare textures, as well as, the volume the sponges will hold.

Moving Water With Basters

3+

Language & Motor development

Math & Science

After the children have mastered sponge squeezing, move to a more difficult task using basters. The squeezing and letting go of the baster is an excellent muscle development activity, which uses more refined muscles than the activity using the sponges. Additionally, it takes some thinking for the children to conclude that they must squeeze the ball and release it underwater to draw the water into the baster. They will discover later that they can do the initial squeezing before they put the baster under the water. It is easier for them to both squeeze and release under the water.

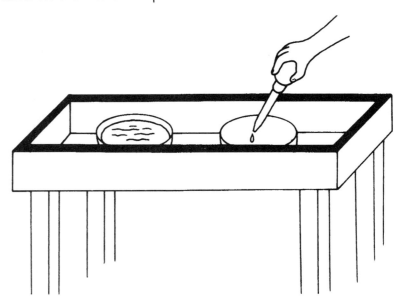

Materials

✓ water table, baby bath tub or dish pans
✓ 2 containers
✓ baster

What to do

Place two containers in the table or tub.

Fill one with water.

The goal is to move all the water from the full container to the empty container by using the baster.

It is a challenge for the children, and they may not be able to empty the full container completely.

Raindrop Race

3+

Motor & Physical development

Math & Science

Once the children have mastered using a baster, try using an eyedropper. The same steps are involved, squeeze, let go and squeeze, but different muscles are involved. The smaller finger muscles come into play.

Materials

✓ water table or baby bath tub
✓ sheet of Plexiglas®
✓ container of blue colored water
✓ plastic eyedroppers or pipettes

What to do

Create a raindrop race. Place a sheet of Plexiglas® in the table or tub.

Give each child using the Center a small container of water colored blue with food coloring and a plastic eyedropper or pipette.

The children draw up the water with the eyedropper and release it on the top of the glass one drop at a time.

Lots of observations are possible when there are several drops "racing" at one time. Their powers of observation are fully engaged to keep track of their raindrops. They learn about speed, surface tension, the joining of two drops and puddles. Try giving each child a different color of water and watch the color mixing.

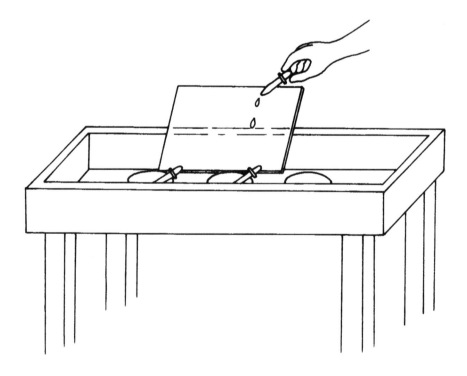

Pouring Corn

3+

Language & Motor development

Dried corn kernels, also known as feed corn, are fun to have in the table or tub. It is inexpensive and it is extremely hard. If you move your Pouring Center outside, there is an additional plus—the birds will make the playground a priority stop for dinner to feast on the spilled corn.

Materials

✓ water table, baby bath tub or dish pans
✓ dried corn
✓ 2 of each size soda bottles, 20-ounce, 2-liter and 3-liter
✓ scissors
✓ colored tape
✓ hot glue gun (optional)

What to do

Fill the tub or table about one-third full of corn.

Make funnels from plastic bottles for this activity. Depending on the number of children, make several funnel bottles. Cut one of each size bottle in half.

Leave the second bottle whole.

Invert the top half of the halved bottle and place it over the top of the matching whole bottle so that the bottle top openings can be joined.

Use colored tape to tape the bottles together. It might help to use a hot glue gun to glue the bottles together before you tape them.

Add the funnel bottles and dry measure scoops to the activity. To make it a little more challenging encourage the children to guess how many scoops it would take to fill each bottle.

When the children are finished with the corn, spread it outside the classroom windows so the children can see the birds eat it.

Sifting Sand

3+

Language & Physical
development

Sand is a pouring favorite. It can be wet or dry. Each offers an entirely different pouring experience. Children are drawn to both.

Materials

✓ water table, baby bath tub or dish pans
✓ sand
✓ plastic sieves, scoops and containers
✓ ice pick or needle (only for teachers)
✓ plastic margarine container

What to do

Fill the tub or table about one-fourth full of sand. If it is not sand manufactured for play, you might want to sift it before using it.

At first, keep the equipment used with the sand simple. Put out a few sieves, scoops and containers.

Make your own sifter by heating a needle or ice pick and piercing a plastic margarine container several times.

To make a flat sieve, pierce several holes in an aluminum pie pan. The children pour the sand into the sieves and catch it in their containers.

Sculpturing Sand

3+

Physical development

Math & Science

Wet sand needs a little more organization. Plan on a way for the children to clean their hands when they are finished. You might want to place a bucket with a small amount of water for the children to use to rinse their hands before they go to the sink to wash.

Materials

✓ water table, baby bath tub or dish pans
✓ sand
✓ water
✓ sand toys, cookie cutters, margarine or yogurt tubs, Jell-O® molds, plastic utensils

What to do

Fill the tub or table about one-fourth full of sand.

Pour enough water into the sand to make the grains stick together, but not runny.

Rather than buying sand toys, use many different kinds of cookie cutters, margarine or yogurt tubs, Jell-O® molds and plastic utensils. Forks make neat animal tracks in wet sand.

The children enjoy cutting the sand with the plastic knives. When they design sand structures, they can use cookie cutters to make decorations on their structures.

Mud

3+

Physical development

Math & Science

Use wonderful, squishy mud but also think about clean up. Perhaps place a bucket with a small amount of water nearby for children to use to rinse their hands before going to the sink to wash.

Materials

✓ water table, baby bath tub or dish pans
✓ dirt
✓ water
✓ small shovels

What to do

Fill the tub or table about one-third full of dirt. For best results, rake and sift the dirt before using it.

Add water to make it very runny.

Give the children small shovels.

Have them create canals and rivers, dams and levees.

Encourage them to figure out how to move the water from one place to another without pushing it along with a shovel.

Confetti

3+

Language & Physical development

Confetti is a great sensory material because of its lightweight compared to other materials. It is also easy to obtain. Ask the parents and friends to save all their paper hole punches.

Materials

✓ water table, baby bath tub or dish pans
✓ confetti
✓ plastic eggs
✓ scale (see directions for making a scale on the next page)

What to do

Fill the tub or table half full of confetti.

Place colored plastic eggs in the tub.

For a little challenge, add a balance scale for the children to use to make measurement comparisons.

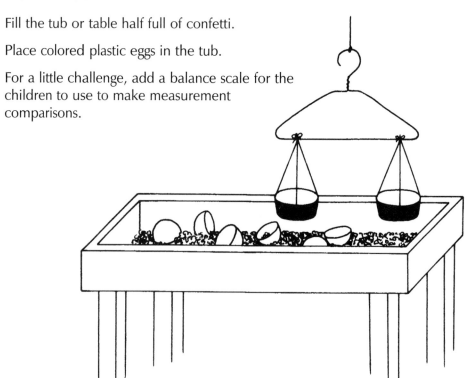

If you do not have a balance scale, make one. Collect two margarine tubs of the same size, string and a coat hanger.

Make four evenly spaced holes around the upper edge of the tubs. Tie four even lengths of string to each hole of each tub.

Take the coat hanger and bend the two sides down.

Tie the four strings to each end so the tubs hang from each end of the bent coat hanger.

Hand this from the ceiling over the work table.

Have the children fill the tubs with confetti until they balance. Have them predict how many scoops it will take to fill the tubs to balance them.

Styrofoam

One way to recycle is to reuse styrofoam peanuts. The texture of styrofoam provides a unique sound when children play with it and it offers diversity and added interest.

Materials

✓ water table, baby bath tub or dish pans
✓ styrofoam peanuts
✓ sand buckets and shovels

What to do

Fill the tub or table about one-fourth full of styrofoam peanuts of different colors and sizes.

Add sand buckets and shovels.

To fill the buckets using the shovels is a difficult task since the peanuts are so light, but the activity encourages the children to focus on control of the material and to be patient.

In the winter time, the children can learn about static electricity since the peanuts, as if by magic, stick to their clothes.

Cornstarch Colloid

3+

Language & Physical development

Math & Science

A colloid is an unusual substance because it is neither a liquid nor solid. It is somewhere in between. Keep a roll of paper towels close by and a trash can. If this activity is done outside, encourage the children to leave the colloid on their hands to see what happens. (The colloid dries to a fine powder and the children can just dust it off their hands.)

Materials

✓ water table, baby bath tub or dish pans
✓ cornstarch
✓ water
✓ plastic utensils (optional)

What to do

Fill the tub or table one-fourth full of Cornstarch Colloid. To make it, mix the same amount of cornstarch and water. It will have a glue-like consistency.

The first few times do not add any plastic utensils. Encourage the children to explore it with their hands only.

When they dig down into the colloid to try to pick it up it feels solid, but as it is picked up it runs through their fingers like a liquid.

Ask the children to describe how it feels on the bottom.

After the children have explored the colloid with their hands, add containers and scoops.

Ice

3+

Language & P)hysical development

Math & Science

Ice adds interest to the Pouring Center. The liquid-solid-liquid cycle is an excellent example of cause and effect based on temperature.

Materials

✓ variety of containers
✓ water table, baby bath tub or dish pans
✓ food coloring
✓ freezer
✓ salt shakers
✓ tongs
✓ gloves or mittens for the children to wear

What to do

Collect a wide variety of containers of all sizes and shapes.

Have the children fill each with water.

Food coloring can be added to the different containers.

Freeze all the containers.

Have the children, wearing gloves or mittens, remove the frozen containers from the freezer and remove the ice from the containers.

Place all the ice in the table or tub for the children to make ice sculptures.

Give each child working in the Center a small salt shaker to shake on the base of their structure to help hold the ice blocks together.

Add tongs for a motor development challenge for them.

Note: If you have a water table with a drain, leave the drain open with a bucket below it. As the ice melts the water drains off and you can replenish the ice frequently during the day.

Shaving Cream

3+
Language & Physical development
Math & Science

Children love the texture of shaving cream. It is a fun "soapy" experience. Wait for a sale, then purchase several cans of shaving cream. This activity is so popular that you will need several cans.

Materials

✓ water table, baby bath tub or dish pans
✓ shaving cream
✓ smocks and a bucket of water
✓ food coloring (optional)

What to do

Cover the bottom of the tub or table with 1" or 2" of shaving cream.

Have smocks for each child and a bucket of water to rinse their hands afterward.

Establish two rules:

Clapping causes shaving cream to fly and it might get into someone's eyes, so no clapping.

Keep hands to yourself when working with the shaving cream.

The children enjoy drawing, squishing and squeezing while using the shaving cream.

To make it more fun, place several bottles of food coloring on a small table close to the shaving cream. The children can add drops of color to their work space and watch as the colors blend.

Soap Sculpture

3+

Language & Physical development

Math & Science

Use soap as an exciting change for the water table. Soap is a fun medium in which to work. Soap can be made as thick or thin as you wish. Here's how to make soap sculptures.

Materials

✓ detergent, such as Ivory Snow®
✓ small container of water
✓ egg beater

What to do

Depending on the size of your work area, pour one or two boxes of Ivory Snow® detergent in the table or tub.

Have a small container of water and an egg beater for each child using the Center.

Allow the children to pour and beat and pour and beat until the soap is mixed well.

If more water is added it becomes slippery and slightly runny. If less water is used it is smooth and stiff.

If the children tire of beating before it is mixed well, use an electric beater to complete the job.

The end result is a squishy, soft, fluffy and pliable material that is easy to sculpt. The children can create all kinds of soap sculptures. The sculptures will dry hard and keep for a long time.

Funnels, Tubing and Sieves

3+

Language & Physical development

Math & Science

Water play is particularly well suited to the development of concepts in mathematics and science. Children learn about empty and full, unit measurement and about the properties of liquids, forces and of surface tension. To do this, put interesting items in the water table: funnels, small pitchers, rubber tubing and sieves.

Materials

✓ water table, baby bath tub or dish pans
✓ funnels, pitchers, rubber tubing
✓ plastic milk jugs
✓ scissors
✓ ice pick (for teachers only)

What to do

Fill the tub or table one-fourth full of water.

Purchase several small funnels, several small pitchers and several 8"-12" pieces of rubber tubing. Make sure the tubing will fit onto the funnel stems.

The children pour the water in the funnels with the pitchers and it travels through the tubing. It is challenging to move the water around the table with the tubing.

For the children to learn about water moving in a different way make sieves to add to the table or tub. Take several plastic milk jugs and cut off the top 2" or 3" from the spout.

Use an ice pick and make multiple holes in the bottom of the milk jug.

When the children fill the jugs the water will spray out of the bottom. Talk about the difference in the tools.

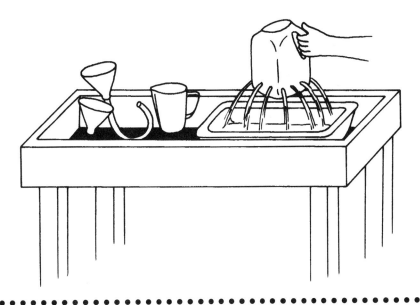

Go Fishing

3+

Language & Motor development

A good way to encourage children to explore letters and numerals is to add them to the water table.

Materials

✓ colored sponges
✓ fishnets

✓ scissors
✓ water table, baby bath tub or dish pans

What to do

Cut letters and numerals from different colored sponges.

Cut out several large rings from large sponges or from a large sheet of foam rubber.

Give the children small, short-handled fishnets to scoop up the letters and transfer them to the center of the rings.

Encourage them to try to write their names with the floating letters.

Also have them try to line up the numerals 1 through 10 by retrieving them with the fishnets and placing them inside the rings.

Exploring Water in Plastic Bags

3+

Language development

Math & Science

Why does an empty plastic bag float on top of the water? Why is it half submerged when water is added? How can the level be changed? What can be done differently?

Materials

✓ water
✓ plastic bags

✓ water table, baby bath tub or dish pans
✓ blue food coloring (optional)

What to do

To encourage children to think inductively and deductively, place several resealable, heavy-duty, plastic bags with different amounts of water and air in them. It might help to put a bit of blue food coloring in the water so that the children can see the water level in the bags, and observe the bags floating at different levels.

The children can open them and add more water, pour water out, wave the bag in the air to trap more air or squeeze out all of the air and water, observing the differences that occur as the bags are floated on the water.

Balls

3+

Motor development

Math & Science

All kinds of additions make the Pouring Center attractive to children. Balls are toys children enjoy. Combining the two, water and balls, invite the children to come and play. The following activity helps develop fine motor skills and hand-eye coordination.

Materials

✓ water table, baby bath tub or dish pans
✓ assorted balls
✓ large sponges
✓ scissors
✓ ladles or scoops

What to do

Fill the water table one-fourth full of water.

Add 10 to 15 balls: ping-pong balls, tennis balls, whiffle balls, golf balls and small soft balls.

Cut several large rings from large sponges or from a sheet of foam rubber.

Float the rings in the water table or tub.

Give each child using the Center a ladle or scoop.

They attempt to scoop the balls up and into the ring.

They observe which will float inside the ring and which falls to the bottom.

Chapter 10

The Science Center

The Science Center is an exciting place where young children manipulate different materials and experience processes used in science. They explore new ideas, building on their knowledge, while doing activities geared to their interest, ability level and experience. The Science Center could also be called the Discovery Center because so much of what the children do leads them to find out new things about the world in which they live—objects, events and people. Because children are active learners, teachers select activities that allow the child to be actively engaged in the activity. In doing so, they learn about their own power to alter things and they begin to understand the limits of their power. Although scientific principles are the main focus of the Center, other new skills are learned—indirectly, naturally, always focusing on the tools used in science—by working with the science materials. Reading, writing, math, measuring, social development, social studies, language development and physical development are just a few areas that are enhanced while working in the Science Center.

Scientific Principles

Young children can grasp many scientific principles provided they are presented at the children's age level and within their interest range. For example, the concept of change is taught at all levels of education. In an early childhood classroom the children might do a color mixing activity, a cooking activity, mix soap and water. Scientific concepts only need to be taught in a developmentally appropriate manner.

Cause and Effect. When a hammer is used to strike a rock and the rock breaks open, the children observe causality, or cause and effect. When children pour water on a plant, allow the plant to have sunlight and watch the plant grow, they are learning that they can influence events and that they and other living things are influenced by events. They learn also that things do not happen immediately; that is, sometimes there is a time delay between an event like watering a plant and the result—a growing plant. In other words, they must acquire patience if they are to notice many of the results of their own efforts.

Patterns. When children look at the cross section of a tree trunk and the life rings are pointed-out, they see the patterns that exists in nature. They may begin to see other patterns, like in butterflies and beehives. When they see inside a cabbage, an onion, a grapefruit and a lemon, sliced across the diameter, they observe more patterns. The most obvious pattern they notice is symmetry. Symmetry is basic to the understanding of modern science.

Cycles. When children observe a butterfly or a chick evolve from a cocoon or an egg, they are learning about the life cycle. When they observe ice melting, water brought to a boil and steam rising from the boiling pot, they are observing the water cycle.

Interactions. When children create a shadow they are interacting with light. When they roll a toy car on a variety of textured surfaces they are interacting with the car; the car is interacting with the textured surface of the road. Children learn that what they act upon, acts upon something else.

Properties. When children pour, scoop and touch, or when they explore texture, color, size and shape, they are learning about the qualities and the properties of things.

There are many scientific principles that we all teach unknowingly, simply by having materials available with activities designed to maximize the children's experiences. Children learn these principles by following four processes basic to science: observing, communicating, comparing and organizing.

When children observe they are seeing, feeling, hearing, smelling and tasting, using their senses. When children communicate they are describing, speaking, recording, writing, researching, reading, drawing, picturing and graphing. Make sure that there are tools and activities available that encourage communication. When they compare they are making general and numerical comparisons by estimating, measuring, weighing and contrasting time with their own action, work or behavior. Since children learn by making contrasts, exploring similarities and differences, select activities that challenge children to make comparisons. Organizing means putting things together in an understandable way. In other words, gathered information must be put together in such a way as to have meaning to the children. Children will also learn to organize information when they seriate, sequence, order, sort, match, group and classify materials.

Language Development

When children describe their research and explain their data, they have a reason for talking. They are talking because it helps them form word-ideas—the centerpiece of thinking about what they are doing. Humans are meaning-seeking creatures. So are young children. They want to make sense of the world in which they find themselves, and they are most motivated when their work has meaning for them. A meaning-based setting is one where children are interested in what is going on to communicate frequently. In reality, they are learning to think and to form thoughts into words.

Reading and Writing

The Science Center is a natural place for reading to occur. Many science books give children the necessary picture or word information they need to do their research. They need to record their data, so it is important that paper and pencil always are available for them. Display charts, graphs and posters for the children to read. Using rebuses (picture directions) to help the children understand how to work activities independently can also be an impetus for reading. Exposing children to print not only enhances reading, but gives them the framework for writing.

Math

Activities in the Science Center teach many math skills. Children work from concrete graphs to pictorial graphs, to abstract graphs as they develop graphing skills. Many activities ask them to estimate the number of items in a jar, days to dry an ear of corn or children with shoestring tied shoes. Other activities explore measuring by length, by weight or in time. Comparing sizes, shapes, colors and amounts all are math related skills. Before children can put numbers in order they have to learn about seriation and sequence. Activities in the Science Center teach these skills. Science and math are so closely interwoven that it is hard to tell where one stops and the other begins.

Physical Development

When children come to the Science Center and choose an activity, work on it and then return it to the shelf, they are refining many physical skills. They are using their sense of balance, for example, to move the activity tray from the shelf to the table. They are using small muscles to manipulate the materials in the activity. They are mastering the movements of their bodies in space when they walk around the people and objects in the Center. If the activity requires crawling, bending or squatting, the large muscle groups are also developed.

Social Development

Whenever children work together on different projects and activities, they are learning to cooperate, share and take turns. Children learn patience when observing and recording an experiment over extended time periods. When children see the results of experiments, they learn that it is important and acceptable to change ther minds when the facts prove that their speculations have been wrong. By working responsibly with materials, animals, insects and ideas from nature, children learn to respect the outdoors. They also learn to respect other children's ideas and work. The Science Center is a place that invites good social skills to develop coincidentally and naturally.

Social Studies

Working in the Science Center also teaches children about people and their jobs. When they do science experiments they are learning what a scientist does. Additionally, activities to complement classroom themes can be placed in the center. A theme on plants, for example, leads to an understanding of the job of a horticulturist, one about rocks helps children understand the role of a geologist.

Creating the Science Center

If children are going to make the best use of the Science Center it must be planned and organized to encourage independent activity by the children. First, create a place where children are in charge of their own learning, in a setting set up to help channel and focus children's actions. Encourage task accomplishment, yet be open-ended. The Science Center should also meet the diverse needs of the children by having activity choices with various degrees of difficulty: some easy, others moderate and still others more challenging.

The location of the Center in the classroom is the first consideration. Since most of the science activities involve the use of sunlight and the observation of weather conditions, a window is important. Clearly define the boundaries of the Center. For example, make one boundary the wall, the second, a bookshelf placed perpendicular to the wall (this will be the shelf where the activities are placed for selection by the children). The third, a smaller bookshelf parallel to the window (allow space for the children to move to and from the shelves) and the back of another center can serve as the fourth boundary. If another center is not an option, make the fourth boundary a strip of hook-side velcro for carpeted flooring or colored tape for tile. What is important about defining the area for the Center is that it says: this is where you and the materials belong if you are using this Center. It organizes and it focuses the children's behavior.

If you have a window, place table and chairs in front of it. This gives the children a well-lit workspace for the activities. Use the window half of the table for plants to be grown. The children select an activity from the shelf, take it to the table to the workspace in front of the plants and return it when they have completed the activity. Use carpet squares if more workspaces are needed. The children get a carpet square to sit on and one to work on, choose an activity from the shelf and work it on the carpet square.

Use trays, baskets, buckets or tote trays to contain all the materials for each activities. This says to the children: this is where the materials for the activity belong and they need to be returned here. Including rebus directions with the activities makes them more child-directed, and it says to children—you are in charge of your own learning. Many of the pictures that accompany the activities in this book can be used to create rebus direction cards. Just use words on the cards that are suitable to your setting and the ability levels of the children.

To provide a good choice of activities for the children, put out two and one-half activities times the number of children using the Center. For example, if four children can use the Center at one time, have ten choices available on the shelves. This seems to be the magic number in keeping children productively and actively involved in what they are doing. If you have too many activities, the children get frustrated feeling they won't be able to get to all of them. They may work too quickly and not enjoy the full benefit of the activities. On the other hand, if you have too few activities, it seems to create a battle zone over who gets which activity and when. Change the activities when the children seem to lose interest in them (if an activity goes unused for several days, it is time to change it). If an activity is popular, however, it needs to remain in the center for as long as it is used. If children are not interested in a particular activity, leave it out for a day to two then put it away. Bring it out 30 days later. You may be surprised at the results. When selecting activities for the center, remember to use what interests the children.

There may be activities that have too many pieces or that are too messy for the children to move from the shelf to the work area. If that is the case, put the activity in front of a chair and tape off a boundary defining the work area. Leave the activity in place until all the children have worked the activity.

To keep the Science Center reasonably clean and tidy, keep a trash can, dry, clean up cloths, a small dust pan, a broom and a moist sponge ready for clean up. This really helps at clean-up time, when the children still should be in-charge.

Using these ideas and suggestions the children's work will be self-directed, and they can discover for themselves what they can learn and what new things they are capable of learning.

Color Making

This is an excellent way for the children to discover things for themselves. It also introduces them to the concept of reversible change.

Materials

✓ yellow lamp oil
✓ blue food coloring
✓ tape
✓ 20-ounce plastic soda bottle
✓ pitcher of water

What to do

Fill the soda bottle half-full of lamp oil.

Mix blue food coloring with water

Fill the soda bottle with the colored water.

Tape the top securely.

Have the children shake the bottle. What happens? The liquid in the bottle turns green.

When they set the bottle aside for a few minutes, the colors separate and the blue and yellow color bands return. The process works for any color lamp oil and a different color water.

Mind Boggling Bottles

Scientific principle: Cause and effect

The major purpose of this activity is to increase children's power of observation and to make discoveries for themselves. They also are encouraged to discriminate and compare objects.

Materials

✓ several 20-ounce plastic soda bottles
✓ yellow crayon shavings
✓ water
✓ yellow tempera paint
✓ yellow food coloring
✓ clear hair gel
✓ liquid detergent
✓ yellow thick yarn
✓ glitter
✓ tape

What to do

In one bottle drop in about 2 tablespoons of yellow, wax crayon shavings. Fill the bottle with water.

To a second bottle, add 1 tablespoon of liquid detergent, 2 tablespoons of water and 1 teaspoon of yellow tempera paint.

Fill a third bottle with water and add a 4" piece of yellow thick yarn.

For the fourth bottle, add 2 drops of yellow food coloring and 1 teaspoon of glitter to 1/4 cup clear hair gel.

Tape all the bottles closed carefully.

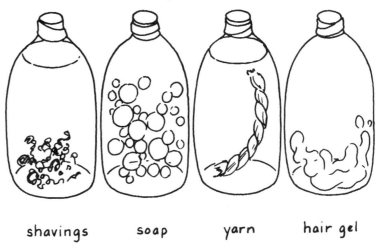

shavings   soap   yarn   hair gel

The children move the bottles by shaking them, rolling them or turning them upside down. They can compare events, time the changes as they occur, count objects suspended in thick fluid and observe how small objects behave in fluids. Other ideas include: put sand, small sea shells and a penny in a bottle, the children are to find the penny; fill a bottle with hay and add a large needle, the children use a magnet to find the needle; add dirt, pebbles and a small, plastic fishing worm in a bottle, the children find the worm.

Wool Washing, Drying and Carding

Science principle: Cause and effect

3+

Language & Physical development

Social Studies

This activity develops and refines small muscle group skills. It also gives the children the foundation for future knowledge about animal coverings and clothing and textures.

Materials

✓ wool (sheared from a sheep)
✓ small washboard
✓ 2 dog brushes
✓ small bottle of cold water detergent, such as Woolite®

✓ 2 dish pans
✓ small squeeze bottle

What to do

Fill the dish pans with 3"-4" of water. One pan is for washing, the other for rinsing.

Put a small amount of Woolite® in the squeeze bottle.

Place the two dish pans in the water table or on a large tray.

The children take a handful of wool, squeeze a little Woolite® on the wool and wash it using the small washboard in the washing pan.

When it is clean, they rinse it in the second pan (you will need to change the water in both pans often).

Set the washed wool aside to dry (outside in the sunlight, if possible).

When the wool is dry, allow the children to card it with the two dog brushes. This takes fine motor skills to accomplish.

Cotton Sorting

Scientific principle: Cycles

3+

Language & Physical development

Social Studies

This activity teaches about raw materials, and how they are used and changed from their original state to serve human needs.

Materials

✓ cotton boles
✓ tray
✓ rebus direction card

✓ colored tape
✓ glue

What to do

Place the cotton boles in the basket.

With colored tape, divide the tray into four sections.

Glue one husk in one section, a cotton seed in another and the cotton fibers in another.

Write small signs to identify the areas with words: cotton, seeds and husk.

Place the basket in the fourth spot.

When a child chooses the activity, he pulls apart the bole and sorts the pieces into the appropriate places. When he is finished, he places all the parts back into the basket and returns the tray to the shelf.

Grinding Corn

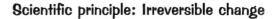

Scientific principle: Irreversible change

3+

Language development
Reading & Writing

This activity introduces the concept of irreversible change. It also reinforces the idea that people must sometimes wait for results and for a task to be accomplished.

Materials

✓ fresh ear of corn (with the husk)
✓ string
✓ roll of adding machine tape
✓ pen or pencil
✓ tray
✓ mortar and pestle
✓ bowl

What to do

Pull back the husk from the ear (without removing the husk).

Tie a length of string around the stem and hang the ear in the window to dry.

Ask each child to predict the number of days it will take for the ear to dry.

Make a chart for the predictions and keep a number line of the days it takes for the ear to dry. Use the adding machine tape for the number line.

The children check the ear each day and write down the number following yesterday's number on the tape.

When the ear is dry, allow the children to shuck the ear, but be sure to go back and check the children's predictions. Then pick off the kernels and place them in a bowl.

Cover the corn with water overnight so the kernels will be soft.

Place the mortar and pestle on a tray with the bowl of kernels.

When a child chooses this activity, she places a few corn kernels in the mortar and grinds them with the pestle until the corn is like mush. When it dries it is powdery just like corn meal.

Note: Purchase wheat kernels and allow the children to grind them in the same way; compare it to the ground corn.

Predicting Jar

Scientific principle: Patterns

This activity encourages prediction and risk-taking (a child must be willing to err if she is to make predictions). The Predicting Jar can be in the Center continuously, only the materials change. The Predicting Jar teaches children that it is okay to guess wrong.

Materials

✓ large, plastic jar with a lid (a smaller one for the younger children). marker
✓ empty box
✓ pencil or marker
✓ small basket
✓ materials to fill the jar such as rocks, marbles, corks, paper clips, buttons, twigs, coins, M&Ms®, leaves, seeds, berries, dog biscuits, nuts
✓ tray

What to do

Write on the side on the jar, Predicting Jar.

Have a small empty box (for predictions), a pencil and a small basket filled with paper on a tray.

Place the tray in the Center along with the predicting jar.

Write on the outside of the box, Predicting Box.

Fill the jar with one material (see list above).

Each Monday, fill the jar with a new material.

The children estimate the number of items in the jar. They make their guesses, write them on a piece of paper and place them in the Predicting Box. They may guess as many times as they like during the week.

On Friday the class counts the items in the jar and checks to see who was the closest to correctly predicting the number of items in the jar.

Caution: With young children who still put things into their mouths, be sure items are large enough so tat they cannot be swallowed.

Color Goggles

Through color goggles children see the world differently. This is a very popular activity.

Materials

- ✓ 6-pack rings
- ✓ red, yellow, blue, orange, green and purple plastic wrap or colored cellophane
- ✓ laminating machine
- ✓ elastic thread and large-eye needle
- ✓ scissors
- ✓ tray
- ✓ rebus card

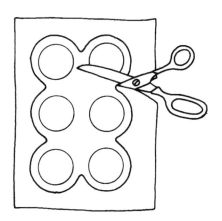

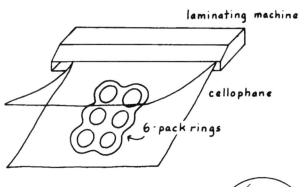

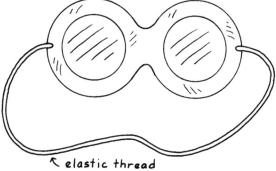

What to do

Make colored goggles in the primary and secondary colors: red, yellow, blue, orange, green, purple.

If you cannot find all the colors, overlap the primary colors to create the secondary colors:

yellow + blue = green
yellow + red = orange
red + blue = purple

Feed the cellophane into the laminating machine, getting it started; then, place the 6-pack rings on the film as it goes through the machine.

If you are overlaying the colors, start one color, overlay the other color, then put the 6-pack ring on the machine.

When you are finished laminating, cut them apart into three pairs of goggles.

Use the elastic thread and a large-eye needle and attach the elastic by threading the needle through each side of the goggles. The elastic holds the goggles in place on the child's head.

Place the goggles on a tray with a rebus card showing a child putting them on.

A child chooses the activity, puts on the goggles and observes the world through the different colored goggles. The child might put on all of them at once or one at a time.

The Shower

Scientific principle: Cause and effect

3+

Language & Social development

This activity really engages children's curiosity and it gets them thinking about cause and effect. The children are always surprised the first time they try it, and they really enjoy introducing it to and surprising others. Listen to their speculations and their hypotheses about why the shower starts and stops.

Materials

✓ 20-ounce soda bottle
✓ heat source
✓ towel
✓ small needle
✓ dish pan

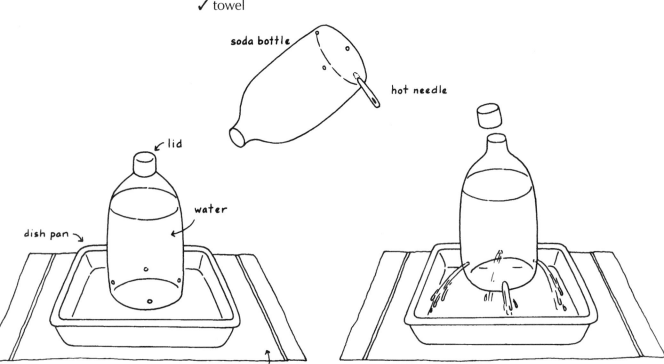

soda bottle

hot needle

lid

water

dish pan

towel

What to do

Heat the needle until it glows red.

Make four small holes in the bottom of the soda bottle.

Fill the bottle with water and screw on the lid, quickly and tightly.

Place the jar in the dish pan on top of the towel.

The child chooses the activity, unscrews the lid, picks up the bottle and observes the water shower raining from the bottom of the bottle.

He screws on the lid again and observes that the shower stops. He may do this many times, trying to figure out why it happens.

When the children have lost interest in doing the activity alone, give them small medicine cups and encourage them to work in groups. One will unscrew the lid and the others will try to catch the water with the cup.

Add food coloring to the water to make it easier to see. The bottle will need to be refilled frequently, since this is such a popular activity.

Magnification With a Water Lens

Scientific principle: Magnification

3+

Language & Social development

This activity encourages fine motor development, and it gives the children many opportunities to explore and discover things for themselves. They gain a sense of independence and autonomy with open-ended activities.

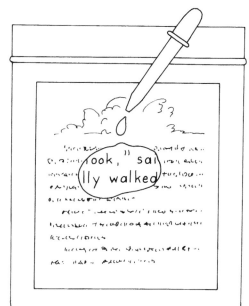

Materials

✓ resealable, plastic bag in different sizes (sandwich, 1-pint, 1-gallon and 2-gallon)
✓ pictures and print
✓ eyedropper
✓ dry cloth or sponge
✓ small container of water
✓ tape
✓ small basket or tray

What to do

Collect pictures and pages with words written on them that fit into the bag.

Place the pictures or print pages inside the bags, close and seal with tape. The bag needs to show pictures or print on both sides.

Place the bags in a small basket on a tray with the eyedropper, the dry cloth or sponge and a small container of water.

A card with the rebus directions can be added to the basket.

The child chooses the activity, takes the tray to the work table and uses the eyedropper to place water drops on the bag.

The child looks through the water at the picture and notices the magnification provided by the water. If the pictures and print are small (difficult to be seen with the naked eye) the fact that a watery medium serves to magnify print medium is made clearer.

She can experiment with all of the different pictures and print. Later when the children tire of this activity, give them magazines, bags and scissors to make their own.

Chimes

Scientific principle: Cause and effect

3+

Language development

Math

This activity lets the children experiment with sound and how they can influence what they hear by how they strike the chimes.

Materials

✓ old headphone set
✓ 3 spoons
✓ 3 forks
✓ string
✓ scissors

What to do

Find an old headphone set from a listening station. It does not matter if it works.

Cut a piece of string long enough so it will attach to both ear pieces and hang down in front of the child.

Tie three forks and two spoons onto this string at 2″ intervals.

Tie each end of the string to the ear pieces (this can be done by attaching the ends of the strings around the headband near the ear pieces).

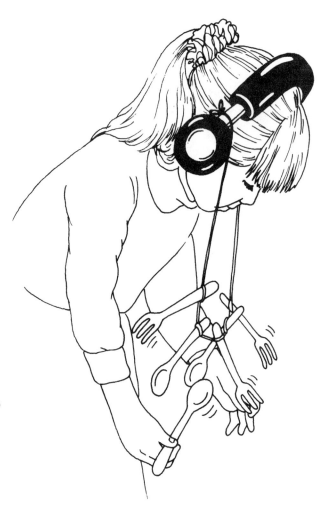

Place the headphone set with the utensils on a tray with the third spoon.

Provide a rebus direction card on the tray.

The child chooses the activity, puts on the headphone set, leans forward so the utensils hang free and strikes the suspended forks and spoons with the third spoon. They are always surprised at the melodic sound they hear and how they can produce some different sounds by the way they strike the utensils.

Spoon Looking

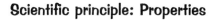

Scientific principle: Properties

3+

Language & Social
development

Children can explore and discover as they work with the same and different reflections of themselves in the bowls of different size spoons. Making comparisons is a natural outcome of this activity.

Materials

✓ variety of highly polished, different size spoons (especially with different size spoon bowls)
✓ tray
✓ mirror

What to do

Place the spoons on a tray with a mirror.

The child chooses the activity, looks at herself in the spoon-bowl and then the spoon-back.

Also encourage her to look at herself in the mirror and see how her reflected image is the same, yet different, in each of the spoons, back and bowl, when compared to her image in the mirror.

Underwater Viewer

Scientific principle: Properties

3+

Language
development

Observing, examining and experimenting are valuable skills for young children to acquire and to develop. The following activity gives them an opportunity to practice these skills.

Materials

✓ 1-pound coffee can
✓ pliers and tape
✓ rubber band
✓ sand
✓ materials such as seashells, twigs or pieces of wood, small pebbles

✓ can opener
✓ clear plastic wrap
✓ dish pan
✓ water

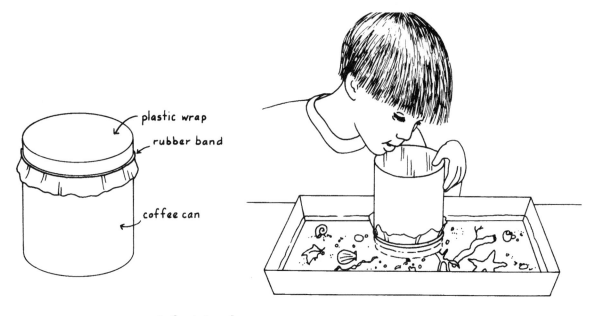

plastic wrap
rubber band
coffee can

What to do

Open the coffee can at both ends. Use the pliers to press down any sharp edges inside the can, cover with tape.

Stretch the clear plastic wrap over one end of the can and secure with the rubber band.

To make the under water world, fill a dish pan with about 3″ of sand.

Add seashells, old wood pieces (or small tree limbs), starfish, small pebbles, rocks and any other ocean related item.

Cover the sand with 6″-8″ of water. Wait for the water and sand to settle.

Place the underwater viewer beside the dish pan so the children can examine the items in the water by looking through the open end of the can and placing the covered end beneath the water surface.

Encourage the children to talk about and describe what they see under the water.

Bird Nest Material Hanger

Scientific principle: Properties

3+

Language & Physical development

This activity introduces children to the scientific method by encouraging them to make a hypothesis, do the research, make observations and compare the concluding results with their original hypothesis. It also develops fine motor skills.

Materials

✓ coat hanger
✓ ribbon pieces
✓ cloth scraps
✓ masking tape
✓ yarn
✓ string
✓ mesh material
✓ basket

What to do

Pull the coat hanger into an oval or a rectangle shape and cover it with mesh.

Tie the mesh at one end of the hanger and tape the other end where the hanger meets the hook.

Put the yarn, ribbon pieces, string and cloth scraps in a basket.

Put the coat hanger with the mesh on it in a tray and place the basket beside it.

The child chooses the activity, selects an item from the basket and threads it through the mesh.

When the coat hanger mesh is full of ribbon, yarn, string and cloth scraps, have the children take it outside.

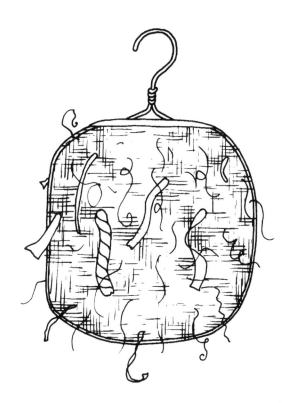

Using the hook end, hang it in a tree for the birds to gather material for their nests. The children can make several hangers for the class, or each child can make one.

This activity is really great for the spring. Use bright colors to attract different birds.

Several weeks later, take a walk around the neighborhood and see if any of the materials can be seen in the nests in the trees nearby.

Car Rolling

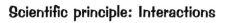

Scientific principle: Interactions

This activity encourages the children to make comparisons.

4+

Language & Physical development

Materials

✓ 3' x 1' piece of carpeting
✓ 3' x 1' piece of poster board
✓ 3' x 1' piece of poster board with sandpaper glued to the surface
✓ 3' x 1' piece of poster board with small pebbles glued to the surface
✓ small toy car
✓ small container

What to do

Put the four types of surfaces on a table.

Put the car in a small container beside them.

The child rolls the car on each surface piece to test the speed of each one.

They compare how easily the car rolls on each textured surface (carpet, smooth poster board, sandpaper-surface poster board and pebble-surfaced poster board).

Add cars of different sizes for the children to test.

Water Drops

Scientific principle: Properties

This is an excellent activity to develop small muscle control and to improve fine motor skills and coordination. It also introduces an understanding about the surface tension of water.

Materials

✓ eyedropper
✓ small container of water
✓ dry sponge
✓ tray
✓ divided tray
✓ food coloring
✓ suction-type soap dish

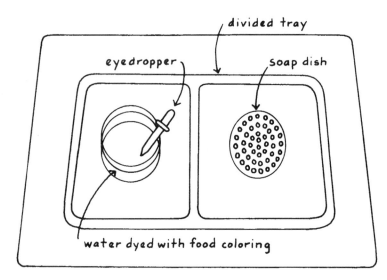

What to do

Put the soap dish on one side of the divided tray and the container of water on the other.

Place the small tray on a larger tray.

Place the eyedropper with the container.

Use the food coloring to color the water.

When a child chooses the activity, she takes the tray to the table and uses the eyedropper to squeeze drops of water into each suction cup without it running over the sides.

When she is finished, she uses the sponge to soak up the water on the soap dish and returns the tray to the shelf.

Tire Pumping

Large muscle control is developed and introductory math skills are explored when children are engaged in this activity. Watch the intensity of some of the children when they fill the tire with air.

Materials

✓ large tire inner tube
✓ old-fashioned hand air pump (the kind that children can stand on, while they pump air into their bicycle tires)
✓ tire pressure inflation-gauge
✓ large tray

What to do

Place the inner tube, the pump and the gauge on a large tray.

The child chooses the activity, takes the tray to an open spot on the floor, connects the pump and pumps up the tire.

When finished, she uses the tire gauge to see how much air has been pumped into the tire. After checking she uses the valve-stem depressor (usually on the opposite end of the tire-gauge) to deflate the inner-tube.

The materials are returned to the tray and she places the tray on the shelf.

Popcorn Weighing

With the following activity, children have opportunities to make comparisons. When children learn that they will be expected to make comparisons, they learn to pay attention more completely to what is going on in the classroom; they learn to focus.

Materials

✓ popped and unpopped popcorn kernels
✓ bowls
✓ 2 scoops
✓ balance scale

What to do

Put each type of popcorn in separate bowls.

When a child chooses the activity, he scoops up the kernels, pours them into the cups of the balance scale and observes which type of kernel weighs more. He makes comparisons. In the process the popped and unpopped popcorn are mixed-up, so put out small amounts at a time. Most of the popped popcorn is eaten.

Have a weighing activity available for the children throughout the year. Weighing really engages the little scientist in most children. Other things to weigh (alternate those that can be eaten with things that cannot): rocks and pebbles, dried fruit slices, coins of different sizes, peanuts, small and large crayons, trail-mix, leaves and twigs, dirt and sand, shells of different sizes and, only for the brave, ice and water.

Pine Cone Experiment

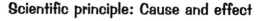

Scientific principle: Cause and effect

This is an excellent activity for children to explore the scientific method, thinking just as a scientist has to think in order to find the right answers. A good activity to do as a group.

Materials

✓ several pine cones
✓ bowl of water
✓ towel
✓ large tray
✓ paper and pen or pencil

What to do

Place the towel on the tray underneath the bowl of water and the pine cones.

When the children look at this activity, one question they might ask is: "What will happen to the pine cone if it is put in the water?"

From this question, the children form a hypothesis: the pine cone will fall apart, turn green, grow into a tree, stay the same (except that it will get wet), the pine cone leaves will roll up like elephant ears or some other prediction.

Write down all of the predictions (so you will not forget). The question and the prediction combined, form the hypothesis.

After predicting, the children move to data gathering. This is the "doing" part of the activity where the children test their predictions. The pine cone is placed in the water and the children observe what happens over time. This might be a time for them to record their observations.

After the pine cones have closed which they will do when they are immersed, the children can arrive at their conclusions.

They can compare the data with their hypotheses. The activity can continue with the question: "What will happen when the pine cone is set aside to dry?"

Tree Book

4+

Language & Social development

Reading & Writing

Math & Science

The children publish their own book in this activity. At the same time, they are learning reading, writing, math and science.

Materials

✓ blank books made from construction paper and plain paper stapled together
✓ camera
✓ string
✓ paper cups
✓ stethoscope, telescope, magnifying glass, minifying glass (optional)
✓ crayons
✓ paper
✓ friendly group of living trees nearby (the children will adopt one of them)

What to do

First the group of children talk about choosing a tree they want to get to know. When the tree has been selected, they will spend several days getting to know it. The book will be about their encounter.

The book begins, of course, with a title page. The page will contain the title, the authors, the illustrators, the dedication, the publisher and the date of publication.

The second page will give information about the tree and a photograph will be placed on the page.

The children will give the tree a name.

They will guess how tall it is, how old it is and how many branches it has.

A leaf can be stapled to page two (it will last much longer if the leaf is laminated).

Page three is for recording the tree measurements. First, how many children does it take to reach around the tree hand-to-hand? Next, measure around the tree with a piece of string, cut it and place it in a resealable, plastic bag. Glue this in the book. Then measure the string in standard measurement units (yards, feet or inches) and record the measurement.

The fourth page is used for recording what the children hear with their ears pressed against the trunk, then with a paper cup held against the trunk. Also use a stethoscope if possible.

Page five is for recording what they see. They look with the magnifying and minifying glass, the binoculars and with their eyes alone. All their responses are recorded in the book.

The sixth page records touch experiences. Take paper and crayons to the tree and do a bark rubbing. Have the children dictate how the bark feels.

The seventh and last page is a class drawing of the tree.

Note: If time allows, each child can select a tree and make a separate book.

Bubble Wands

4+

Language & Physical development

This is another cause and effect experience for the children, best done outdoors. It helps them appreciate the forces of wind and to understand what wind can do.

Materials

- ✓ Bubble Formula: 1 part water to 3 parts liquid detergent
- ✓ blowing tools: six-pack rings, strawberry baskets, embroidery hoops, coat hangers and straws
- ✓ mesh material or used nylon stockings
- ✓ tape
- ✓ dish pan
- ✓ basket

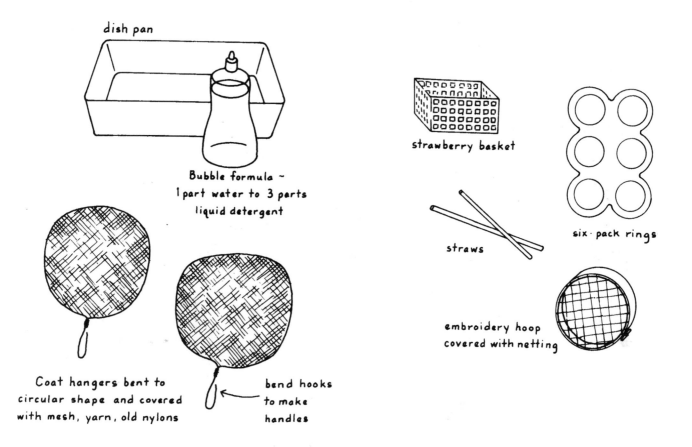

dish pan

Bubble formula ~
1 part water to 3 parts
liquid detergent

strawberry basket

straws

six-pack rings

embroidery hoop
covered with netting

Coat hangers bent to
circular shape and covered
with mesh, yarn, old nylons

bend hooks
to make
handles

What to do

Make several types of coat-hanger bubble wands. Bend a coat hanger into circular shape and cover it with mesh or fine netting (mesh and netting usually are used to package plastic Easter eggs or bagged, citrus fruit sold at the grocery store). To make very small bubbles, cover the coat hanger with a nylon stocking.

Shape the netting to the coat hanger by feeding the material over the hanger, toward the hook end. Tape the material around the hook end and shape the hook into a handle.

Wrap the hanger with yarn (to hold a large amount of the bubble mixture) to make very large bubbles. Fold the hook, as mentioned before, to make a handle. Instead of a hanger try an embroidery hoop.

Move a table outside to have a place for the activity. Place on the table a dish pan one quarter filled with the bubble mixture. Put two berry baskets, two six-pack rings and two straws in a basket beside the bubble mixture.

The child chooses a blowing tool and uses the mixture to make the bubbles.

Place a large low-sided container one-quarter full of the bubble mixture on the table. Beside it place a basket with the premade bubble wand coat hangers or embroidery hoops.

When a child chooses this activity she selects a tool and makes the bubbles.

Soda Bottle Terrarium

Scientific principle: Cycles

4+

Language development

Social Studies

The children must follow sequential directions to complete this activity. Sequencing and patterning skills are two important developmental tasks that need to be mastered by young children in order to read. By the way, the soda bottle terrarium makes a great Mother's or Father's Day present.

Materials

✓ 1-liter soda bottles with green or black bottoms (bottoms of bottles are flat and base can be removed as discussed)
✓ hair dryer   ✓ scissors
✓ baskets   ✓ small pebbles
✓ small container   ✓ soil
✓ scoop   ✓ dish pan
✓ small plants   ✓ tray
✓ water-spray bottle (to be used for misting the plants)

What to do

Use a hair dryer and heat the glue spots between the base and the body of the bottle. Wave the blowing air around the bottle to soften the glue. When the glue is softened, pull off the base. You will now have a black tub with holes in the bottom. Place it aside.

Cut off the stem and the mouth of the bottle (later this will be used as the terrarium top).

Separate the components by placing the terrarium bases in one basket, the terrarium tops in another.

Put the soil and a scoop in a dishpan, the pebbles in a small container and the plants and spray bottle near the activity in the Science Center.

Use a tray to define the workspace for the child when making the terrarium.

The child chooses this activity, selects a terrarium base and a terrarium top from the baskets and places them on the workspace tray.

He puts a handful of pebbles in the base and scoops soil on top of the rocks, almost filling the base.

He plants his plant and mists it with the spray bottle.

He places a terrarium top over the plant and pushes it down between the soil and the terrarium bottom.

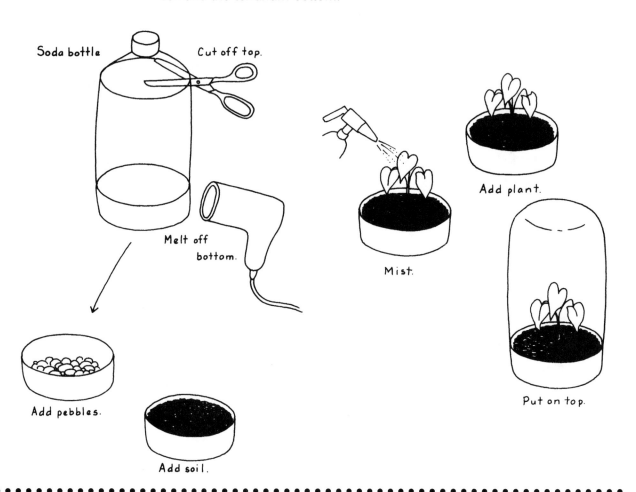

Soda bottle Cut off top.

Melt off bottom.

Add pebbles.

Add soil.

Mist.

Add plant.

Put on top.

Mirror Work

5+

Language development

Math

This activity is excellent for presenting the concept of symmetry to older children in a way they will understand. Part/whole relationships are also explored.

Materials

✓ rectangular mirror, approximately 5" x 7"
✓ tape, if needed   ✓ cards of illustrations below
✓ scissors   ✓ glue
✓ tagboard   ✓ self-adhesive paper or laminating film
✓ basket   ✓ tray

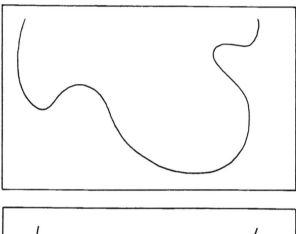

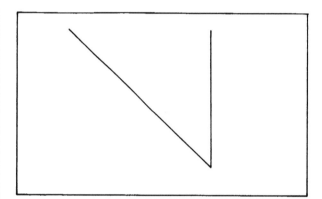

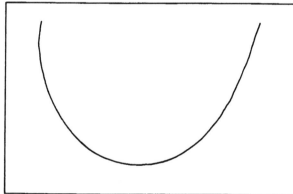

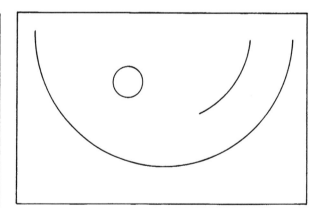

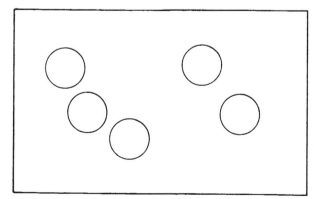

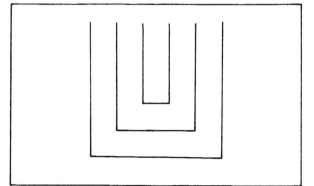

What to do

If the mirror does not have a protective frame, then tape the edges carefully.

Copy the following illustrations.

Cut out each card, glue it to tagboard and laminate it for longer life.

Place the mirror and the cards in a basket.

Put the basket on a tray.

A child chooses the activity, manipulates the card in the mirror to make the picture whole, smaller, longer, slanted or invisible. When he is finished exploring the activity, he replaces it on the shelf.

Note: Encourage the children to make their own cards to use with the mirror.

Chapter 11

The Woodworking Center

Working in the Woodworking Center is a pleasure for young children. They feel responsible and trustworthy when they use adult tools in the center with care and respect. Combining young children and woodworking requires planning, organization and training, but it can be safe. That is not to say that there are not going to be some minor injuries—a small cut on the finger, a finger hit with a hammer—but these can be incurred in any environment. You might ask, "But, why take the risk?" When a child learns that he is trusted by the adults around him, he develops a strong sense of self. He is practicing the assumption of responsibility.

The Woodworking Center is not about making a finished product. Making a finished product is not important or even desirable—the children need to feel free just to experience hammering, sawing, screwing and drilling. When they have experienced these things and understand the mechanics of the tools, then they can pursue nailing two boards together, or creating a construction from their own blueprints.

Language Development

Reading and writing can occur as a direct result of the activities that take place in the Woodworking Center. The children can make signs using index cards to title or label their construction. By having premade blank storybooks available children often are inspired to write stories about their construction. In the Woodworking Center children must work in a sequential order for an activity to be successful. In so doing they are practicing sequencing skills necessary for reading. They also create patterns with nails, observe patterns in the grain of the wood and repeat patterns when they copy another child's construction. Understanding patterns is a necessary foundation for reading.

Math

Many math skills are learned in the Woodworking Center. For example, one-to-one correspondence (one bottle cap for one nail), fractions (the piece is cut into three pieces) counting (how many nails or pieces of wood are needed) and measuring using standard units—inches and nonstandard units—bottle tops, string, paper clip chains (how many bottle tops wide is the board). They learn about sizes and shapes—circles, squares, rectangles, angles and ovals—when using tools and wood.

Physical Development

The first thing the children learn about is safety. They learn about the tools and how to use them correctly and safely; how to care for them. Proper care is important because rusted, dull, broken or bent tools are dangerous when used.

Science

As children work with wood they discover things about wood properties like grain, hard wood, soft woods, color, characteristics (knots), splits and splinters. They learn about irreversible change when they saw a piece of wood apart. They experience cause and effect when they drive a nail into the wood with a hammer.

What about wood scraps?

The first source is parents. Many parents do woodworking projects at home and might have leftover pieces. Also ask for parents' assistance. Usually they are delighted to help. Inquire about scraps at building sites, lumber companies and cabinet shops. If you tell them why you are asking, people usually are happy to assist. If your school district has a maintenance shop, they probably use a lot of wood and may save the scraps.

What's the best wood to use? Pine, Spruce, Fir and Poplar are all good, but Pine is the softest; it is the easiest for a child to hammer and saw. Stay away from Cedar (many splinters) and treated lumber (very hard and it splits in long jagged pieces that can be dangerous).

Creating the Woodworking Center

Here are helpful tips to make the Woodworking Center safe and successful:

✓ Purchase safety glasses or goggles and insist on their use.

Have corks for the children to stick on protruding points of nails. For example, if the children drive the nails through the wood and they protrude from the other side, the children can glue the corks in place over the protruding nail. Using the corks to cover protruding nails is also a safety consideration when children carry their wood constructions home.

✓ Have plastic grocery bags near the Center. Children put their finished constructions in the bags to carry them home. If they wrap up their constructions and then put them in their backpacks, there is less damage to the construction.

✓ Keep a dust pan, a small broom and a trash can near the Center for ease in clean up.

✓ Use rebuses (step-by-step picture directions) as much as possible. They show the children how to use the various materials and equipment properly. These simply drawn pictures invite the children to read along and to work at their own pace. Many of the illustrations that accompany the activities in this book can be easily converted into rebuses by adding written directions to the pictures. Consider the ability level of the class when adding the words.

Safety

Start simply. The most important consideration in the Center is safety. To ensure that the children become safety conscious and that they have respect for the Woodworking Center, they need to be carefully trained about tool use. Place a hammer, a container of large headed nails and a large wood block (for nailing into) in the Center. Introduce one tool at a time. Make sure the children understand the use of each tool and that they practice the safety rules for each one as they are introduced. Have the children brainstorm a few rules that apply to each tool so they have a feeling of ownership for the rules. This makes the rules easier for them to follow. When each tool is first introduced make sure that you are free to offer more supervision until you feel the children respect the tools.

The following rules are suggested:

✓ One child at a time in the center.

✓ Before starting work, put on protective eye glasses or goggles.

✓ When using the hammer, tap lightly when starting a nail. The nail can be hit harder when it stands firmly in the wood. (It is firm if it won't wiggle side-to-side when you try to move the nail.)

✓ Only a nail or the wood should be hit with the hammer.

✓ When using the saw, keep both hands on the saw at all times. Hold the wood in place with a vice or a C-clamp. Only the wood should be sawed with the saw.

✓ When using the drill, drill only into the wood.

✓ When using the screwdriver, keep both hands on it at all times.

✓ Screwdrivers are used only to turn screws into the wood.

✓ Screwdrivers are not for prying up pieces or for separating one piece of wood from another. This can be very dangerous and other tools are needed for this purpose.

✓ Check the tools when you are finished. Be sure they are clean and put away properly.

✓ Clean up after yourself.

Woodworking Board

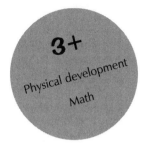

3+

Physical development

Math

Storing the tools in a manner that is safe and accessible is always a consideration for the Woodworking Center.

Materials

✓ large sheet of plywood or pegboard
✓ markers
✓ 1 large headed nail
✓ hammer

What to do

Make a tool storage board by attaching a large sheet of plywood to the wall.

Before attaching it trace each tool that will be used in the center on the plywood board and color in the outline to create a silhouette. Place large headed nails in the appropriate places so that the tools can be hung over the silhouettes.

If you prefer using a pegboard with hooks to hold the tools, be sure to use a hot glue gun to hold each hook in its place on the pegboard.

After the children have learned about each tool separately, have them choose a tool from the board, use it and return it to the board.

Tool boxes are useful if the only tools are hammers and nails. If other tools are used the children can cut themselves while searching for a tool in the box.

Accessories

3+

Language & Physical development

Math & Science

Many skills can be learned in this Center, but the greatest skills of all are those acquired through children's own exploration of simple objects—odd things and safe adult tools that are in the Woodworking Center.

Materials

✓ wood glue
✓ C-clamps, sheets of sandpaper, measuring tools and other safe tools
✓ box
✓ markers, pens, paper, cardboard scraps

What to do

Have a box of woodworking accessory tools on the work bench or close to the work area. Include wood glue, several C-clamps (1, 2 and 3″ sizes) and several sheets of sandpaper (fine and medium grit).

The children glue small wood pieces together, glue objects before they nail them and smooth rough spots on the wood.

Place measuring tools of all kinds in a box: short rulers, foldout rulers, tape measurers and nonstandard measuring tools (jar tops, bottle caps and string). This invites math skills to develop.

Place markers, pencils, paper and cardboard scraps in the box for writing.

Sometimes a building needs a sign, a plan needs to be drawn or a message needs to be conveyed to the next worker. All of these are a reason for reading and writing in a meaningful way.

These center additions enhance children's skills in observation, comparison, symmetry and balance.

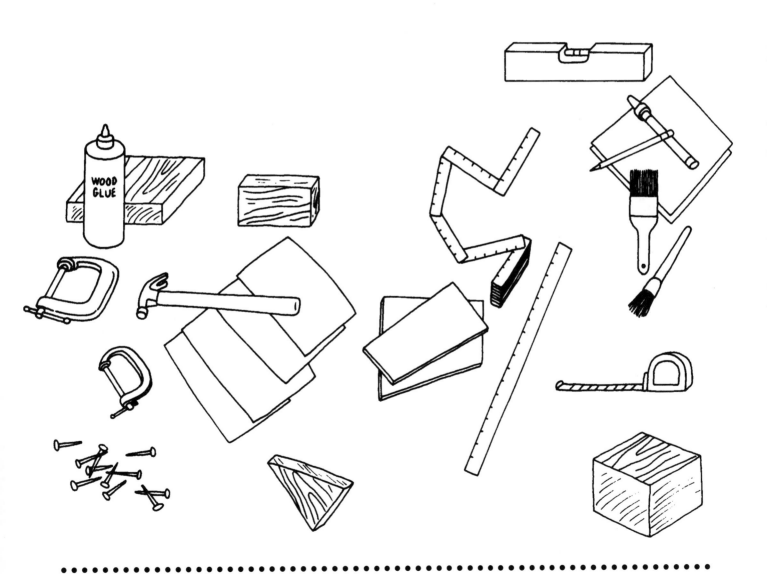

Golf Tee Construction

3+

Physical development

Science

Three or four year olds enjoy woodworking activities; however, many are not ready to handle a hammer and nails. The following activity can be used to introduce woodworking. Move on to more difficult tasks when the children are ready.

Materials

✓ soft headed mallet
✓ large quantity of golf tees, preferably the longest ones
✓ several large pieces of styrofoam

What to do

Have the children use the mallet to hammer the tees into the styrofoam.

As an alternative to styrofoam you can use an empty fabric cardboard bolt.

Hammering

3+

Physical development

Science

Children develop hand-eye coordination when they try to hit a nail on the head.

Materials

✓ large headed nails
✓ hammer
✓ large block of wood

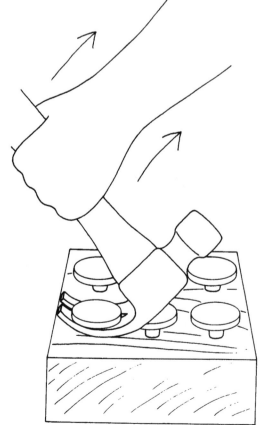

What to do

Prepare this activity for the children by nailing many large headed nails 1/4"-1/2" into a large block of wood. (Roofing tacks are great.) With a hammer, have the children drive the nails into the wood block.

Demonstrate how to use the claw of the hammer to pull out the nails.

Encourage the children to pull out the nails they have hammered into the wood.

To challenge the children further, talk about the claw being a lever and see if they can describe how it works.

Note: Copy the two illustrations below and display in the Woodworking Center. This will give the children a visual reminder of how to hammer and remove the nails. (This is a rebus or picture direction.)

Using Spools

3+

Physical development
Science

Very young children with all ability levels enjoy the thrill of hammering nails. For children who need help getting nails started, this is a perfect activity for them.

Materials

✓ long large headed nails
✓ hammer
✓ spools
✓ large block of wood

What to do

The nails selected should be able to pass through the hole in the spool, so that the spool can be removed from around the nail once it is secure.

The spool holds the nail in place while the children get the nail started in the block of wood.

When the child can no longer hammer the nail, because it is level with the top of the spool, the child removes the spool and continues to hammer the nail into the wood.

Bottle Caps

3+

Physical development

Math & Science

Bottle caps are a good example of things that can be recycled.

Materials

✓ bottle caps
✓ hammer

✓ nails
✓ wood block

What to do

Have the children nail bottle caps into the wood block.

This is a very popular activity, so be sure to gather a large supply of caps.

The children can create some interesting designs with bottle caps on their construction.

Sponges and Wood

3+

Physical development

Science

Often it is hard for children to nail two boards together. This requires an attention span longer than most of them possess at this developmental stage. Children sometimes quit in frustration. Offer this activity as an alternative to nailing two boards together.

Materials

✓ sponges
✓ nails
✓ large blocks of wood

✓ scissors
✓ hammer

What to do

Cut sponges into 1" squares.

Have the children nail the sponge squares into a piece of wood.

The children will still have to figure out which nail will go through the sponge and into the wood. They will use the same techniques they would in nailing the two boards together, but they can complete the task and be successful in a shorter time.

Corks will work as well as sponge squares, but they have a tendency to tear. Include both materials if possible.

As the children's skill increases, nailing two boards together becomes easier.

Wood Scraps

4+

Physical development
Math & Science

When the children have mastered hammering, move to construction.

Materials

✓ box of wood scraps
✓ assorted nails
✓ hammer

What to do

Add a box of wood scraps to the Center.

The children try to nail two boards together.

Have a variety of lengths of nails available so the children have to do some problem solving to figure out which nail will go through the two boards. The short nails will not and the long ones go too far. (This is where the corks, mentioned in the introduction, are used to cap protruding nails.)

It takes time for the children to plan ahead, measuring the nail and the wood, to select the proper length nail.

Wood and Wire

4+

Physical development
Science

When the children are ready for more complicated tasks in the Woodworking Center, add materials or change how they are used to keep the children's interest. One way to do this is by adding colored wire. This is found inside all kinds of premanufactured telephone cable or telephone wire. Split the exterior cable surface with a knife and small plastic coated colored wires will be visible and easily removed.

Materials

✓ short lengths of colored wires, from TV cable company or telephone company
✓ hammer
✓ nails
✓ large blocks of wood

What to do

The children hammer nails into wood and use the wire to twist, wrap or thread around and about the nails.

Wood and Paper

4+

Language & Physical
development

Math

This activity encourages letter, number or geometric shape recognition.

Materials

✓ paper cutouts of letters, numbers or shapes
✓ nails
✓ hammer
✓ blocks of wood

What to do

Add paper cutouts or old letters cut for bulletin boards that are no longer in use. Any type of paper cutouts will work.

The children make their construction by nailing letters, numbers or shapes to it. This opens the door for talking about the cutout.

Use cutouts that relate to a theme, such as transportation—cars, trucks, boats, planes, trains. It is a great way to get the children talking about the topic.

Wood and Paint

4+

Language & Physical
development

There are times when movement between Centers allows a child to carry a more involved project to completion.

Materials

✓ wooden construction
✓ paint
✓ paintbrushes

What to do

Children enjoy painting their constructions.

This can happen in two ways. First, the children can take their woodworking to the Art Center and paint it there.

Second, a small area can be set up close to the woodworking bench with a tub of paint and a brush.

Offering a selection of colors is important in encouraging children to make choices.

Wood and Leather

4+

Physical development

Science

Different textures can invite the children to create a new kind of wood construction.

Materials

✓ leather scraps—hard and tanned pieces
✓ basket
✓ nails
✓ hammer
✓ large blocks of wood

What to do

Soak the hard leather pieces in water so that you can cut them into small pieces. When they dry they will become hard again.

Put all the leather pieces in a basket on the woodworking table for the children to use to decorate their constructions by nailing them onto it.

Don't stop with leather. Add netting, silk, burlap and other textured material.

Colored Nails and Shapes

Sometimes older children need a new challenge or a new idea to renew their enthusiasm.

Materials

✓ nails
✓ spray paint in several colors
✓ hammer
✓ several large blocks of wood
✓ markers

What to do

Spray paint about 200 nails different colors by lightly nailing them to a board and spraying them with enamel paint.

Allow the colored nails to dry.

Collect several boards and draw a different geometric shape on each one. For example, start with a circle drawn in blue on the board. Then have the children hammer blue nails around the blue circle. Have a single geometric shape on each board on which the children hammer the corresponding colored nails, or they can create a colored nail design within the given shape.

After the children have mastered this activity, make it more complicated. Draw several shapes on one piece of wood like a purple circle overlapping a red square, with a blue triangle overlapping both. The children then nail the corresponding nail colors to the geometric shape. After the children have mastered this figure ground work, place markers, pieces of wood and colored nails in the Woodworking Center for the children to create their own designs.

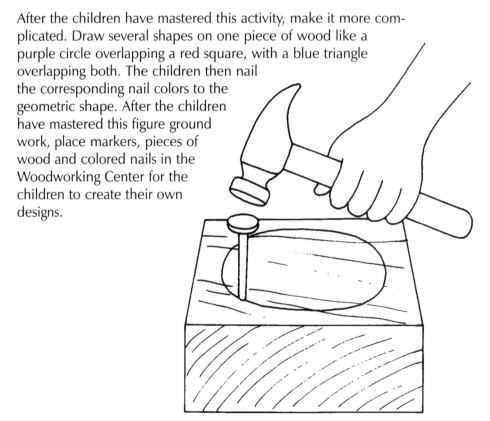

Crowbar

4+

Physical development

Science

Removing nails from wood is a difficult task. This is as much a part of construction as hammering. If the children misapply a nail, they will want to move it. If they hammer nails into a board that is not for taking home, then as a part of their job, they need to remove the nails.

Materials

✓ block of wood with nails hammered into it
✓ hammer
✓ small crowbar
✓ masking tape

What to do

One way to remove nails is with the claw end of the hammer, but this may not be the best way. The claws on lightweight hammers are often too thick to get beneath the embedded nail head; and, getting the right leverage is hard.

If children are having difficulty with the claw, try using a small crowbar that is made for removing nails.

Cover the end that is not for pulling out nails by wrapping it with several layers of masking tape creating a pad, or cut an opening in an old tennis ball and force it onto the end of the crowbar. Use a little hot glue to help it adhere.

The handle is padded so that children do not hit themselves in the face in the nail comes out suddenly.

Teach the children to slip the nail removing end under the nail and press down.

Set up a nail removing training board on which the children can practice until they have mastered the skill.

Wood, Nails and Rubber Bands

4+

Physical development

Math & Science

Making music or making a game can be part of the Woodworking Center.

Materials

✓ hammer
✓ nails
✓ block of wood
✓ assorted rubber bands

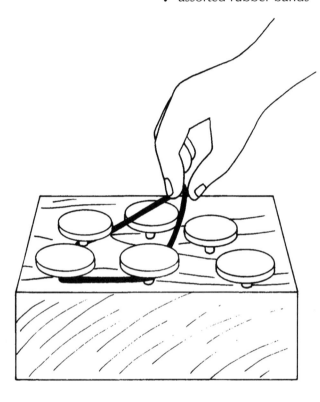

What to do

When the children are at a loss as to what work to do in the Center, which happens now and then, encourage them to hammer nails into a board part of the way. This in itself is challenging.

Place a variety of rubber bands in the Center.

Have the children explore music and sounds by stretching the rubber bands over the nails and plucking them like musical strings.

They can also make a geoboard game. Have them stretch different rubber bands on the nails in different geometric shapes.

Ask them to encourage a friend to match their shape with a different color rubber band.

Brads and Woods

4+

Physical development

Science

Sometimes it is frustrating for children to nail objects to constructions because the objects are small and odd shaped. Gluing may appear to be the only way to attach objects to their constructions. There is an alternative, however.

Materials

✓ brads
✓ hammer
✓ block of wood

What to do

Purchase fasteners from the hardware store that look like large staples; they are arch shaped and pointed on each end. They often are called brads. They can be purchased in different sizes.

These are more challenging to hammer but will offer the children a way to nail twigs and other bulky objects to their constructions.

To add a new perspective, explore hammering the brads into the wood half-way, leaving a loop on which shoestrings can be tied.

Have the children weave a design with the shoestrings that have been tied on the exposed loops. They can create with an exciting variety of weavings on their own.

Junk and Wood

4+

Physical development
Science

When the children have mastered simple wood construction projects, they will be looking for something new to spark their interest and encourage creativity.

Materials

Assorted objects, such as

✓ washers	✓ buttons
✓ feathers	✓ zippers
✓ ribbon	✓ twist ties
✓ wheels	✓ marbles
✓ dowels	✓ keys
✓ rulers	✓ clothespins
✓ game pieces	✓ twigs
✓ popsicle sticks	✓ washers
✓ jar lids	✓ tongue depressors
✓ paper clips	✓ glue
✓ tape	✓ nails
✓ hammer	✓ string

What to do

Collect a variety of junk objects that the children can glue, stick, nail or tie to their constructions. See the above list.

Collect these items during the school year.

Add them to the Woodworking Center, step back and watch what happens.

Sawing

5+

Physical development
Science

Sawing has a big attraction for the children, especially the older ones, but it has the potential to be dangerous. Training children to use the saw is very important.

Materials

✓ saw, preferable a miter box saw
✓ vice grip or large C-clamp

What to do

If you have a work bench with a vice to hold the wood, just tighten the jaws tightly, start the cut with the saw (about 1/4" deep) and give the child the saw.

Use a miter box saw as it is smaller, has fine teeth and it has a square blade tip. It is easier for the children to manage. It requires a little more muscle control, however.

Make sure children understand to keep both hands on the saw at all times and to keep the saw in the cutting groove.

If you do not have a vice on a workbench, use a large C-clamp to hold the wood to a table. Make sure the wood protrudes from the table so there is no danger of the children sawing the table.

If you are using a large wood block for the work table, then nail the board to be sawed securely to the wood-block work bench.

Suggestions: To cut down on friction heat, use a soap bar and run it carefully down the saw blade teeth. Before storing the saw for the summer, rub a bit of machine oil over the blade. Use a little machine oil on all the tools and rub them with a soft cloth.

Drill

Using a drill is a difficult task for the children to undertake and it is best done by children with some woodworking experience. Also, before attempting to use the drill, give the children lots of practice with an egg beater in the Pouring Center. The hand drill is easier to use than the bit and brace drill. For obvious reasons, power tools of any description are not to be used.

Materials

✓ large block of wood
✓ hand drill

What to do

To start, give the children a large block of wood and the drill. Demonstrate how to put the drill bit into the jaws of the drill. Before the children arrive, use a hammer and nail and make small holes in the block of wood. The children will use these as a start for drilling.

They hold the drill handle in one hand and turn the crank with the other.

The children move from hole to hole experimenting with the drill. When they have it mastered they can drill all the way through small boards.

Note: The boards should be no more than 1/2″ thick try to use white pine only.

Screwdriver

Using a screwdriver is also a difficult task. It is best used with more advanced woodworkers. The screwdriver may slip out of the screw head and could cut the child's hand. Encourage the children to keep both hands on the screwdriver.

Materials

✓ large block of wood
✓ screws
✓ screwdriver

What to do

With the younger children, it works well to have screws already started in a large board. The children can screw and unscrew the screws at will. It is easier and less dangerous because the screw path (vertical) has been established by you.

When you feel the children have reached a skill level when they are ready to move on, encourage them to drive a start-hole in a board with a hammer and nail before starting to screw. The children will also enjoy using a Phillips screwdriver.

Note: Use white pine wood and reasonably new screws with large, flat heads.

Index

Squish, Sort, Paint & Build

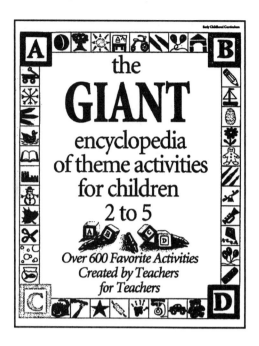

The GIANT Encyclopedia of Theme Activities for Children 2 to 5

Over 600 Favorite Activities Created by Teachers for Teachers

Edited by Kathy Charner

A nationwide contest with thousands of entries produced this large book. There are 48 themes filled with more than 600 teacher-developed activities that work. From the alphabet and art to winter and zoo there are themes for every season and every day of the year.

All activities are clearly described and ready to use with a minimum of preparation. This is an ideal resource for a busy teacher. The book has a special strengthened binding which allows it to lie flat on a table. 512 pages.

ISBN 0-87659-166-7
Gryphon House
19216
Paperback

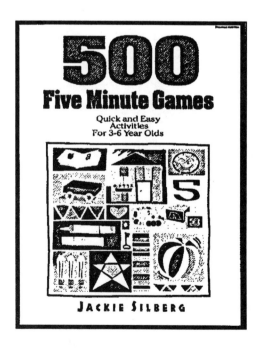

500 Five Minute Games

Quick and Easy Activities for 3-6 Year Olds

Jackie Silberg

Enjoy five-minute fun with the newest book from the author who brought you the popular series **Games to Play with Babies, Games to Play With Toddlers** and **Games to Play With Two Year Olds**. These games are easy, fun, developmentally appropriate and promote learning in just five spare minutes of the day. Children unwind, get the giggles out, communicate and build self-esteem as they have fun. Each game indicates the particular skill developed. 270 pages.

ISBN 0-87659-172-1
Gryphon House
16455
Paperback